ABINGDON MARRIAGE MANUAL

Copyright © 1974 by Abingdon Press

Library of Congress Cataloging in Publication Data

BIDDLE, PERRY H.   1932-
  Abingdon Marriage manual.

  Bibliography: p.
  1. Marriage. 2. Marriage service. 3. Marriage law—
United States. I. Title.
BV199.M3B52   264′.5   73-21799

ISBN 0-687-00484-5

MANUFACTURED BY THE PARTHENON PRESS AT
NASHVILLE, TENNESSEE, UNITED STATES OF AMERICA

For Sue, in gratitude;
For Lindsay and Perry, III, in hope

PREFACE

The purpose of this book is to give the working pastor assistance in the planning and conducting of the wedding service, guidance and resources for developing an effective ministry to couples *after* as well as before the wedding, help in developing church policy regarding weddings and receptions, and a convenient collection of current wedding services from several denominations and perspectives. In addition, state laws regarding marriage are provided.

When I was invited by Abingdon Press to write a replacement for the well-known *Cokesbury Marriage Manual,* I was both delighted and overwhelmed. But I have been thrilled by the enthusiasm and cooperation of many friends, old and new, who have helped make this book a reality. Pastors of local congregations, couples, denominational consultants in worship and church music, professors of pastoral theology, and friends who are interested in liturgical renewal and in helping make marriages more creative and joyful have been of invaluable assistance. Space will not permit listing them all.

I owe a very special debt to the following for their valuable counsel on developing a ministry to couples: Dr. William B. Oglesby, Jr., Professor of Pastoral Counseling, Union Theological Seminary, Va.; Dr. Seward Hiltner, Professor of Theology and Personality, Princeton Theological Seminary; Dr. Wayne E. Oates, Professor of Psychology of Religion, Southern Baptist Theological Seminary; Dr. Liston O. Mills, Professor of Pastoral Theology and Counseling, Vanderbilt Divinity School; and Dr. Theron S. Nease, Professor of Pastoral Counseling, Columbia Theological Seminary.

I am indebted also to the following for assistance regarding the theology of worship, history and nature of wedding liturgies, and current wedding practices: Dr. Paul W. Hoon and Dr. Tom A. Driver, Union Theological Seminary, N.Y.C.; Dr. Marion J. Hatchett, Professor of Liturgics and Music, School of Theology, University of the South; Dr. James C.

Barry and Dr. R. B. Easterling of The Sunday School Board, Southern Baptist Convention; the Rev. Hoyt Hickman, Board of Discipleship, The United Methodist Church; the Rev. Darrell B. Ray, University Chaplain and Director of Religious Affairs, Vanderbilt University; Dr. Tom B. Martin, Dr. Robert H. Crumby, and the Rev. Richard Baldwin, pastors of congregations in Nashville; and to the Rev. D. "Pat" McGeachy, Director of "A New Song" and a pioneer in the current liturgical renewal movement.

The chapter on music and the wedding was made possible largely through the constructive criticism of Dr. James R. Sydnor, Professor of Church Music, Presbyterian School of Christian Education, and three ministers of music for local congregations, Mr. Billy J. Christian, Mr. Charles Merritt, and Mr. Hal Hopson. Mr. Hopson read the working draft and offered very valuable suggestions.

For new insights into and personal appreciation for the value of growth groups I wish to thank Dr. Howard J. Clinebell, Jr., Professor of Pastoral Counseling, School of Religion, Claremont, California; Dr. James W. Angell, minister, Claremont Presbyterian Church,

Claremont, California; Dr. Chris Meadows and Dr. John A. Wilson, Vanderbilt University; and the Tuesday evening class in group dynamics and process of the Vanderbilt Divinity School.

I am indebted to Mr. Tim Manor, a friend and student at the Vanderbilt Law School, for preparing the section on state laws regarding marriage.

I wish to thank the Rev. Frank Robert, librarian of the Vanderbilt Divinity School library, for assistance in research and Dr. Harold W. Fildey, Professor Emeritus, Vanderbilt Divinity School, for very helpful suggestions at each stage of manuscript preparation.

Dr. John Killinger, Professor of Preaching in the Vanderbilt Divinity School, has inspired me through his own prolific writing, encouragement, and warm friendship. I am particularly indebted to him for his contribution of "A Free Service for Weddings," (p. 197 ff).

Finally, I wish to express gratitude to my parents, without whose constant faith and abiding love for each other this book would not have been possible.

Perry H. Biddle, Jr.

CONTENTS

PART I

MINISTRY BEFORE AND AFTER THE WEDDING CEREMONY

The church and its clergy have a unique opportunity to prepare persons for marriage and to offer a follow-up ministry in the months and years after the wedding. The proclamation of the biblical message of God's judgment and grace and the administration of the sacraments are channels of God's gracious mercy to individuals and to couples. In the fellowship of believers forgiveness and love are received and given. There a new quality of life is experienced. The concern of the people of God for others can be expressed in a very significant way through a ministry to persons before and after the wedding ceremony.

Many forces are at work shaping the lives of those preparing for marriage. Some are positive. Others are negative. Family life is one of the more important of these forces. Christian family life is the *most* important of all. In the family where Christ is central, persons learn how to live, love, and function as husbands and wives from the examples of their parents.

The economic, social, and political as well as religious forces in society affect the preparation of persons for marriage. For example, the liberation of women (especially economic) has radically changed traditional roles in marriage and society. A woman no longer seeks marriage or must remain married in order to find security and to be accepted in society.

The wise pastor will become more aware of these forces at work shaping the lives of old and young alike as they prepare for marriage or live as husband and wife. He* will recognize the limitations and strengths of the ministry which he and the church can offer. Through participation in continuing theological education and other educational opportunities, the concerned pastor will seek to keep abreast of developments in pastoral ministry, especially as they relate to marriage and the family.

In recent years great emphasis has been placed on the importance of premarital counseling. It has been advocated as a means of

---

* The common pronoun "he" will refer to either male or female persons except when specifically used for males only.

launching couples onto the sea of wedded bliss with greater odds for happiness. It has been taught as a means of reducing the rising divorce rate, creating a more stable family life, and insuring the future of the monogamous marriage. Many couples expect premarital counseling. Most secular wedding planning guides mention premarital counseling by the pastor as an item not to be overlooked in planning for the wedding.

But authorities do *not* agree on the value, if any, of premarital counseling. Opinions of professors of pastoral counseling range from those who say premarital counseling comes at the most educable time of life to those who say that it is practically useless, a matter which will be dealt with later in the chapter.

But every minister who marries a couple engages in some form of ministry to them before and after the ceremony. The crucial question is: What kind? Some clergy, with or without the concurrence of their congregation's governing body, require a minimum of three premarital counseling sessions. A recent study of the premarital ministry offered by a sample group of United Methodist pastors revealed that 94 percent offered some form of ministry before marrying couples. Roughly two-thirds met once or twice with couples. One-third met three or four times to give premarital counseling.

But there is growing dissatisfaction on the part of some pastors and other professionals with premarital counseling as it is currently practiced. The ministry *after* the ceremony is being stressed more than in the past. One professor of pastoral counseling says that most couples are not receptive, unless they come at their own initiative and seek specific help before getting married, to the kind of premarital counseling that most ministers seem duty bound to provide.

Another professor of pastoral counseling is even more pessimistic about the value of premarital counseling. He says that in recent years he has come to believe that it is practically useless. By the time the young couple comes to the minister, they seem impervious to anything that may be said or done, although they will agree to practically any proposal that the minister makes.

During courtship individuals lose most of their judgment. By definition, persons "in love" are in such a dizzy state that they become reckless. The problems of marriage are not noticed or considered. Occasionally, the bride and groom know that they are marrying the wrong persons, but they are in such a passion and are being driven so hard by the applause of society that they cannot help themselves. One weepy young bride hysterically insisted on backing out of the wedding three minutes before the ceremony began. But the wedding caterer persuaded her to go through with it! If this is the case, what ministry, if any, can a concerned pastor have to couples preparing for marriage?

Often there is another subtle but very real obstacle to a ministry through premarital counseling: the opposing assumptions held by the couple and the pastor. The engaged couple asks their minister to marry them because they have finally reached a common decision that they are ready to be married. But the minister, guided by much of the current literature on premarital counseling, may assume that there is something "wrong" with the personality factors of the man or woman, and some "static" is assumed to exist in their communication with each other which needs to be eliminated. The literature challenges the minister to uncover these difficulties and, through the proper premarital counseling technique, to heal them and their relationship before marrying them.

But unless the minister can persuade the couple to set aside their assumptions and adopt his, then premarital counseling cannot take place. And to attempt to so persuade them is to play God!

Couples may shy away from premarital counseling because of the negative connotations of "counseling" and the fear of invasion of privacy. "Preparation for marriage ministry" is a better term, and its use should be encouraged.

A good rule of thumb to follow in conducting marriage preparation interviews with couples is: *Don't assume anything!* In the interview the pastor should attempt to create an open, trusting, and supportive relationship which will continue after the wedding. In fact, some ministers feel that this may be the most valuable aspect of such interviews. And through posing the right questions the minister can gain greater knowledge about the couple and the ways in which he and the congregation can minister to them now and later.

For example, unless you know the couple well, do *not* assume that neither has been married and divorced one or more times. And it should not be assumed that they hold to traditional values and attitudes about marriage and premarital chastity.

Knowledge of previous marriages or of an already existing intimate relationship will allow the minister to provide a more appropriate ministry than otherwise. Careful, sensitive listening by the minister to the couple will provide clues he can follow up. This can be done without prying, probing, or invading privacy —much as a physician follows up clues to an illness in order to offer healing.

Each minister inevitably develops his own style of ministry for preparing couples for marriage. The alert, creative, and caring pastor will continue to reshape this ministry. While a program of interviews, books, tests, etc., may evolve, the pastor will be ever seeking to improve the ministry he offers.

Three goals for the initial premarriage interview might be the following:

1. To determine whether or not the minister can, in good conscience and according to the rules of discipline of his denomination, participate in this event.

2.   To offer a series of two or three additional conferences, if the couple desires, in order to (a) assist them in clarifying the terms of their marriage contract, (b) review the meaning of Christian marriage and particularly their vows, and (c) discuss the rehearsal and ceremony itself.

3.   To set up a series of conferences either with the couple alone, or with other couples, after the ceremony for "on the job training" in marriage.

During the initial interview the minister should be able to determine how many additional conferences will be desired before the wedding. But this question may be left somewhat open. If the minister can in good conscience marry the couple, he will check his schedule to make certain the dates for both rehearsal and wedding are open. And he will ask them to clear these dates with the church office, church organist, custodian, and other personnel. He will also have discovered if both are of legal age to be married without parental consent. If they are not, he will ask for conferences with any parent(s) who objects to their marriage. Even when the couple is of legal age it is advisable to have a conference with any parent(s) who does not favor the marriage.

If either party has been married previously, the pastor will be especially sensitive to needs which may be expressed. Whether a previous marriage ended in death or divorce, the minister will want to offer individual counseling in order to enable the man or woman to work through any negative feelings still existing which might affect the new marriage. James G. Emerson, in his book *Divorce, The Church, and Remarriage,* sets forth his criterion of "realized forgiveness" in regard to the remarriage of divorced persons. The pastor counseling with persons who are divorced but are preparing for remarriage will find this a very helpful resource. Should either party be divorced, the minister may want to consult with an advisory committee appointed for this purpose by his church's governing board or judicatory.

If the couple accepts the pastor's offer to meet with them for additional interviews in preparation for marriage, he should schedule the next meeting before concluding the first interview. These conferences will be aimed primarily at helping the couple clarify the terms of their marriage contract and gain a better grasp of the meaning of Christian marriage.

One highly recommended book on marriage counseling outlines the following marriage preparation interviews:

Interview One

The minister sees each partner separately to discuss their romance, their common interests, their relationships to both families, their understanding of sex, and the planning of family. While one is being seen, the other, if he desires, can take the Schedule E. [Uncovers feelings regarding the marital relationship. Available from: 3828 Locust St., Philadelphia, Pa.] The couple are asked to see a physician.

Interview Two

The minister sees the couple together to discuss their budget, their planning of a home, and the values by which they live. He asks them to bring in a simple budget as a basis of discussion for this session.

Interview Three

The minister sees the couple together to discuss their interests, how they resolve conflicts, and their adjustments to difficulties. The latter part of the interview is used to discuss the religious side of marriage with the marriage ritual as the focus of discussion.[1]

The author, who is a recognized authority in marriage counseling, advocates flexibility in the use of this proposed schedule. The pastor should allow for the individual differences among the partners and for the uniqueness of their relationship.

A significant recent development in the ministry of preparing couples for marriage is *group premarital seminars*. One such program was offered on a university campus by a University Common Ministry composed of six denominations including Roman Catholic. A modest fee was charged each couple to cover costs of materials and honoraria for speakers. The major areas of concern in marriage were presented by speakers or films and then discussed in small groups led by clergy. The seminars were offered on six successive Sunday evenings for two hours. A similar program could be offered by an individual church or group of churches each year, or more often.

[1] Charles William Stewart, *The Minister as Marriage Counselor* (Nashville: Abingdon Press, 1970), p. 61.

In support of this approach one authority says that *group* premarital counseling is one of the most promising movements to aid young people to prepare more adequately for marriage. A professor of pastoral counseling affirms that a great deal can be accomplished in group premarital counseling which cannot be accomplished with couples alone. He writes that ideally the church should make both experiences available to couples. Lyle B. Gangsei's book, *Manual for Group Premarital Counseling,* offers concrete suggestions for planning such a ministry. Other helpful materials will be found in the annotated bibliography at the end of this manual.

The clergyman seeking to strengthen his ministry to couples preparing for marriage would do well to read selectively in the literature currently available. Then he should shape a program which corresponds to his abilities, interests, time available, and the needs of those who come to him to be married. While recognizing the limitations and opportunities in this area of ministry, the caring pastor can continue to offer a supportive and educative ministry to those willing to accept it.

A Ministry After the Wedding Ceremony

The pastor's and the church's ministry to persons before and after the wedding are not two separate ministries but simply two phases of a single ministry. The follow-up ministry, rather than premarital counseling, is being recognized as the more crucial of the two by many pastors and other professionals.

A well-known professor of pastoral care says that while he thinks postmarital counseling is more critical than premarital counseling, he does not think this eliminates the necessity for premarital counseling. After the wedding ceremony the couple is more open and a great deal can be accomplished in the weeks that follow. This fairly recent emphasis in pastoral care recognizes the crucial nature of the first few months of marriage when the terms of the marriage contract are being negotiated and husband and wife roles are being shaped.

Two of the classical writers on this subject of the period just passed, Fishbein and Burgess, claim that most marriages are made permanent or are lost in the first two or three months. Recognizing the crucial importance of the early months of marriage Howard Hovde has written *The Neo-Married* to assist in providing an effective ministry to couples recently married. Hovde points out that although the third year of marriage is often considered the hardest because most divorces occur at that point, the time involved in deciding to divorce and going through the procedures to divorce indicates that the primary trouble year is the first. It is during the early months of their married life that couples develop the patterns of behavior that they will follow later. How successful they are in this early period will greatly affect the rest of their married life.

Collaborating this position, Tom McGinnis in *Your First Year of Marriage* argues that the first year of marriage is *the* crucial one. During this time individual and marital patterns of feeling, thinking, and acting are developed which tend to persist. These patterns, says McGinnis, determine to a large extent how happy and successful one's marriage will be. As one of America's foremost marriage counselors, McGinnis says that the first year of marriage may well be the most exciting and challenging year of your life.

For too long pastors have emphasized premarital counseling but neglected a ministry to couples *after* the wedding ceremony. Having pronounced them man and wife and having signed the wedding certificate, the pastor often allows them to fade into the church's woodwork to struggle alone through the crucial and formative first months of marriage. He may drop by for a social visit. Or he may call to recruit the husband or wife for church membership or participation in the young adult church school class.

The minister of one of America's best-known pulpits reveals what is probably true in most churches today. "I have no particular strategy for post-wedding counseling," he writes. "If the couple is a part of the life of the parish that one is serving he will be able to stay in touch." But more than staying in touch is needed to enable couples to develop growing, vital, satisfactory marriage relationships. A creative, vigorous, and continuing ministry by the clergy and church is called for if the challenge is to be met.

There are many excellent resources to enable the pastor and congregation to develop such a supportive ministry to newlyweds. A series of cassette tapes with printed guides by Howard J. and Charlotte H. Clinebell is one of the best refresher courses for clergymen in growth counseling. The subjects which would be most helpful in providing a ministry to the married are: "Leading a Marriage Growth Group"; "Highlights of a Marriage Enrichment Workshop"; "Using Marriage Problems for Growth"; and "Enhancing Sexual Intimacy in Marriage." [2]

If the pastor elects to have a series of conferences with the couple alone rather than lead a group seminar on marriage he will have greater flexibility in shaping the conferences to meet the particular needs of the couple. Two books mentioned earlier, *The Neo-Married* and *Your First Year of Marriage,* are excellent resources for structuring a series of marriage conferences with a couple. The newlyweds might be asked to read one or both books. Another recent book which commends itself for use in post or prewedding ministry is David R. Mace's *Getting Ready for Marriage.* Written by a leading marriage counselor, this book is designed to give marriage preparation to couples who may not have access to formal counseling by a professional. It would be an

[2] Howard J. and Charlotte H. Clinebell, *Growth Counseling: New Tools for Clergy and Laity* (Nashville: Abingdon Press, 1973).

excellent book to put into the hands of a couple who are unable to meet for postwedding conferences.

There are four group oriented programs which can be adapted for offering a postwedding ministry. All four are biblically sound and make use of the best insights from the human sciences. A request for further information and names of representatives in your area will enable a pastor and governing board to consider any or all of their programs. They are as follows:

1. National Presbyterian Mariners, 8353 West 70th Place, Arvada, Colo. 80002
2. Yokefellows, Inc., 19 Park Rd., Burlingame, Ca. 94010
3. Faith at Work, 1000 Century Plaza, Suite 210, Columbia, Md. 21043
4. Association of Couples for Marriage Enrichment, Bowman Gray School of Medicine, Winston-Salem, N. C. 27103

One local church formed a group for newlyweds called "The Ring and the Book." The name came from the poem by Robert Browning. The group sought to combine the values

of marriage and faith in a growth group. While
it had the usual social dimensions—suppers,
outings, etc.,—it also included intimate sharing of selves, expectations of mates, marriage,
life, book reviews, and studies in the field of
personal relationships and family life. Occasionally the group went on a weekend
retreat.

Two recent books especially suited for use
in such a group are *Meet Me in the Middle*
by Charlotte H. Clinebell and *Till Divorce Do
Us Part* by Lofton Hudson. The first book is
written in light of the women's liberation movement and asserts that it is the woman who
must take the intiative to change the balance
within the marriage relationship. It is a radical
application of freedom to the dilemma of the
modern woman. Hudson's book gives valuable
help in building healthy, open, growing marriage relationships.

Some limitation may need to be placed on
membership in such groups if they are to serve
their purpose. One group agreed that a couple
graduated from the group when their first child
arrived. Others limit membership to couples
married five years or less. Others limit the
combined ages of the couple.

Programs for such groups usually revolve around the major concerns of marriage. Often local doctors, bankers, investors, ministers, and marriage counselors are asked to speak and lead discussions on a topic. Or programs may be led by members of the group.

A newlywed group might form a book discussion fellowship and supper club. The pastor or a couple may coordinate it. A different couple is asked to give a book review, and the group joins in discussing the issues raised. Several current bestsellers on marriage could be used such as *Open Marriage* by the O'Neills, *The Intimate Enemy* by Bach and Wyden, *The Spouse Gap* by Lee and Casebier, *The Mirages of Marriage* by Lederer and Jackson, or *The Intimate Marriage* by the Clinebells.

Howard Hovde in *The Neo-Married* suggests the following topics for a newlywed group. One or more sessions may be given over to each topic.

Session	1	Introductory
Session	2	Marriage as a covenant
Session	3	Family finances
Session	4	In-laws

Session 5	Sex and family planning
Sessions 6, 7	Communication as speaking
Session 8	Expectations
Session 9	Love
Sessions 10, 11	Learning to listen
Session 12	Your marriage and the church
Session 13	Life goals

The church committee responsible for family education may elect to offer an annual marriage workshop led by a professional marriage counselor or professor of pastoral counseling. Or a professional counselor might be engaged to lead a series of seminars for newlyweds each year with a modest fee charged each couple. Many young adults are taking advantage of adult education opportunities for which they pay a fee. The church is missing an opportunity to make a marriage enrichment program possible if it does not offer courses, free or for a modest fee, from a Christian perspective. A fee may attract more couples and insure more faithful participation.

Other ministries to couples after the wedding are waiting for the imagination of the pastor and church to discover and implement. Joseph E. McCabe in *The Power of God in a Parish Program* tells how one church developed a more creative approach to marriage. In chapter seven he describes the process by which a church studied the problem of the secularization of the wedding service and discovered ways to do something positive about it. This included a ministry to the couples.

In conclusion, any ministry before and after the wedding ceremony should be an expression of the church's concern, not merely the concern of the pastor. Ordinarily the pastor will take a leading role in developing this ministry. But the congregation and governing body should be involved in planning and carrying through on plans. Otherwise the program will be viewed as the current pastor's "baby" to be thrown out when he leaves, if it doesn't die earlier for lack of support.

Your congregation is looking to you, its pastor, to initiate ways in which you as pastor and people can render more effective ministry to couples before and after their wedding.

MAKING THE WEDDING
SERVICE MORE PERSONAL

In recent years there has been an increasing interest among couples preparing for marriage in writing either part or all of their wedding service. Some have involved family and friends in creating a wedding festival complete with balloons, folk music interspersed with parts of the wedding ceremony, and colorful and unique costumes. But the more usual personalizing of the wedding has consisted of writing vows which are said to each other, involving the congregation in readings of scripture and poetry, congregational singing of processional and recessional hymns, and joining in litanies composed for the occasion. And there have been varying degrees of modification of the traditional wedding liturgy.

The pastor will find some of the guidelines set forth in this chapter helpful in planning and performing ethnic weddings. Since customs vary greatly between ethnic groups, it is beyond the scope of this book to deal with them individually.

While there have been a number of books published to provide resources and guidance for the couple in composing their wedding service, little has been written to guide the minister in the process of working with such couples. The present chapter attempts to meet this need.

If the denomination's liturgy for the wedding service permits some leeway in the content and way it is conducted, and most do, then the minister must decide whether or not he is willing to venture forth with a couple who wishes to create their own unique service. If he is willing, he can let this be known in the church's manual on weddings and receptions and in the first counseling interview with couples preparing for marriage.

More often than not, couples who will approach the minister with a request to assist them in writing their own wedding service are secure in their own sense of self-identity and social status. Such couples have a sincere desire to express their own unique feelings and values in their ceremony.

When such a request comes there are several

factors which must be considered: the denomination's teaching regarding the meaning of
marriage, the denomination's liturgy, the time
available for the couple and minister to work
together on a service, the openness of both
sets of parents to anything other than the
traditional wedding service, and the minister's
own willingness to spend additional hours in
counseling interviews and in planning for the
personalized wedding. There needs to be a
systems approach in the process of helping
a couple write their service since there are
many persons and factors involved which affect each other and the total outcome. The
couples' families, the church, and the community at large have a vested interest in the
success of this rite of passage which the
couple plans.

If the couple does not have sufficient time
to read, research, reflect, and work with the
minister in writing their own service, then the
minister should insist that they choose one
of the classical, contemporary, or free services.
However, even these services allow some
flexibility and freedom in the selection of
music, scripture, wedding homily, Communion, gestures, etc.

One campus chaplain requires five pre-marital interviews with any couple desiring to write their own wedding liturgy. The process of writing the vows and putting together the various parts of the wedding ceremony can be a very useful counseling technique since it demands that the prospective bride and groom think through the meaning of their marriage commitment in greater depth than they would otherwise. Throughout the process of assisting the couple to write their wedding service the minister should retain an influence over what is proposed. And he should retain the freedom to refuse to conduct the service if he feels that innovations proposed will alienate the couples' families from them or otherwise be destructive of their marriage.

The wise pastor will keep the plans being proposed by the couple in the perspective of the overall view of their marriage and the meaning such plans, if executed, might have for them many years later. In the intensity of emotion and the excitement of their romance the couple may overlook this lasting effect of the wedding service.

Wedding liturgies, like other liturgies, may be classified as (1) classical, (2) contempo-

rary, and (3) experimental or "free-wheeling."
Examples of the classical service are the
services of the Episcopal *Book of Common
Prayer,* the Presbyterian *Book of Common
Worship,* and *The Book of Worship* of The
United Methodist Church.[1] Such forms retain
the formal traditional style with the traditional
words and gestures. Examples of the contem-
porary wedding service are the "Celebration
and Blessing of a Marriage" [2] in the *Services
for Trial Use* of the Episcopal Church, the
"Order for the Public Worship of God: The
Marriage Service" [3] from *The Worshipbook* of
the Presbyterian Church, "The Marriage
Service," [4] prepared by the Inter-Lutheran
Commission on Worship, and "The Marriage
Service" [5] conducted by Dr. Wayne E. Oates,
an example of a Baptist wedding service.

The experimental or free-wheeling service
is the one which the couple writes or borrows
elsewhere. The wedding service prepared and
conducted by Dr. John Killinger is an example

[1] See page 117.
[2] See page 133.
[3] See page 187.
[4] See page 150.
[5] See page 126.

of the experimental wedding service.[6] Its variations are infinite.

For many couples a contemporary wedding liturgy will provide the framework for the wedding liturgy they create. Written in contemporary English, using modern images and more recent theology of marriage, the contemporary service lends itself to use by couples who want to break with the classical service but who either do not wish to venture into creating an experimental or free-wheeling liturgy—or who may be prevented by time or other factors from doing so. The contemporary service, for some, will be an adventure into the unfamiliar and risky area of liturgical innovation. For others, accustomed to contemporary worship services, it will seem familiar and comfortable.

Obviously the couple wishing to create a free-wheeling wedding service will need to be prepared to spend time in becoming familiar with the development of the wedding liturgy, the theology of Christian marriage, and in reflecting upon what they want to say in and through their service. Such a service should

[6] See page 197.

have a unifying theme and liturgical integrity. Few couples are able, for various reasons, to do their homework in preparing an experimental wedding liturgy. For this reason very few such services are liturgically outstanding. While they may be festive and fun, they may appear in the light of years to be more like a circus than a religious celebration (and there is a difference). *Joyful dignity* can be attained in an experimental wedding liturgy, but only through careful reflection and planning.

There are two trends in recent wedding liturgies which should be encouraged especially. They have good support in the tradition of Christian wedding liturgies, and their revival is commendable. They are: active participation on the part of the congregation and wedding party in the service and the incorporation of the proclamation of the Word and celebration of the Eucharist.

During the first three centuries of the church a civil marriage of baptized Christians was considered a Christian marriage. Tertullian (c. 160-220 A.D.) admonished Christians to celebrate the Eucharist at marriage services as a substitute for the Roman custom of sacrificing to Jupiter. For the first thousand years Christians followed secular customs but infused them with Christian meaning. Marriage was not officially designated a sacrament by the Roman Church until 1439 A.D. Protestant couples should be encouraged to plan their wedding services so that Christ is exalted, God is recognized as the giver of life, love, and marriage, and the unity of believers with one another and their God is celebrated. The wedding which includes the Word and Eucharist is the ideal pattern.

When a wedding homily or sermon is included this should come early in the service, before the betrothal. The Communion should be celebrated as the climax of the wedding service, with the wedding ceremony itself serving as the "hinge" on which the whole service of worship turns. The homily may be given, and usually is, by the minister. But another member of the wedding party may be asked to do this. Scripture regarding marriage may be read by members of the wedding party or congregation. The bride and groom may read passages to each other, especially passages selected from the Song of Solomon.

The wedding homily should set forth the biblical understanding of marriage. The most

important texts regarding marriage are: Gen.
1:26-31; 2:18-25; 3:5-7, 15-20; and Jesus'
teaching in Matt. 19:5-15; Mark 10:2-16;
Luke 16:18; and I Cor. 6:15-20; 7:1-40; II
Cor. 11:2-4; Eph. 5:21—6:4; Rev. 19:6-16.
Other biblical passages in which the marriage
symbolism is used to convey the mystic relation between God and his people are Song of
Sol.; Isa. 54:5 ff; Jer. 31:31 ff; Hos. 2; John
2:1-11; 3:29.

In the Bible marriage is understood as
founded by God. It is a vocation. Men and
women are called of God to be husband and
wife and parents. In this sense marriages are
made in Heaven, although a particular marriage may not be. What God has joined together (the male-female relationship in marriage), mankind is not to put asunder.

In Matt. 19:4-6, Jesus reaffirms sexuality
as part of the goodness of creation. He declares that the union of man and woman in
their total being as "one flesh" is at the core
of marriage. The wedding sermon should not
be so "spiritual" that it denies this aspect of
marriage.

The covenant character of marriage should
be affirmed in the wedding homily or elsewhere

in the service. As a holy covenant Christian marriage implies a freely chosen, unconditional, lifelong, exclusive relationship. It cannot be stressed too strongly that marriage is based, not on romantic love, but on an *act of the will*. Emil Brunner says that while marriage cannot be based on love, natural love has been made an essential part of the order of marriage by God. He writes:

It is true, of course, that marriage springs from love, but its stability is based not on love but on fidelity. Through the marriage vows the feeling of love is absorbed into the personal will; this alone provides the guarantee to the other party which justifies the venture of such a life companionship.[7]

There is no place in the Christian tradition for what is called "term marriage" or "experimental marriage" (this is different from an experimental *liturgy*). Such marriages lack the most essential element of marriage—the obligation to be faithful. Marriage is primarily the personal concern of two people who love

[7] Emil Brunner, *The Divine Imperative* (Philadelphia: Westminster Press, 1947), pp. 357-58.

each other, who feel drawn to each other by love for one another and who express their feeling for each other by saying: "With you alone do I wish to be united, wholly, and as long as we both shall live." This vow to be faithful frees the partners to create an open, trusting relationship not bound by an overconcern for their subjective feelings toward each other. Any attempt to modify permanence in marriage vows, implicity or explicity, should be vetoed by the minister. A vow to live as husband and wife as long as we both shall "love" instead of "live" implies a less than Christian understanding of marriage.

The couple and minister may want to read some wedding homilies to gain ideas for making the wedding more meaningful. Arthur M. Vincent has edited a book of addresses and worship aids for church weddings entitled *Join Your Right Hands*.[8] A wedding homily need not be long and dull! R. M. Redder has created a delightful wedding homily celebrating marriage in poetical form.[9] Another very

[8] Arthur M. Vincent, ed., *Join Your Right Hands* (Saint Louis: Concordia Publishing House, 1965).

[9] *The Christian Ministry*, 2 (Nov., 1971), 17. (Order from The Christian Century Foundation, 407 S. Dearborn St., Chicago, Ill. 60605).

helpful model wedding sermon is Dietrich Bonhoeffer's "A Wedding Sermon from a Prison Cell." [10] The wedding homily is an opportunity for the minister to venture in using other forms than the usual "three points and a poem" sermon.

The wedding ceremony follows the Word proclaimed and is a response in action and words to God's gracious action and Word in Jesus Christ. The covenant which bride and groom make with each other is a commitment to love one another in response to God's steadfast love revealed in Christ. Agape, unselfish and unmerited love, is the quality of love they are to share.

The Eucharist climaxes the wedding service. It is truly a thanksgiving for God's gracious gift of marriage, for these two persons who have now entered the marriage relationship and for God's providential guidance and care. In the Communion Christ comes anew to renew the faithful. In the breaking of bread and pouring of the cup God's covenant with his people is re-enacted and renewed. And the

[10] Dietrich Bonhoeffer, *Letters and Papers From Prison* (New York: Macmillan, 1967), pp. 25-32.

steadfast love of God is given afresh to bride and groom to enable them to continue loving and forgiving each other as God loves and forgives them.

Most couples are not clear about what makes for a Christian service of worship. Since many weddings resemble a social "coming out" ceremony or another revolution of *The Eternal Bliss Machine,*[11] couples planning their own ceremony will need guidance from the minister.

Several recent books can be helpful at this point. Paul W. Hoon's *The Integrity of Worship*[12] is one of the best studies in liturgical theology available. It is "must" reading for the minister who has more than a passing interest in worship. It will give a couple who is seriously interested in creating an experimental wedding service much of the background and insight into worship which they need. *New Forms of Worship*[13] by James F. White will

[11] Marcia Seligson, *The Eternal Bliss Machine* (New York: William Morrow & Co., Inc., 1973).

[12] Paul W. Hoon, *The Integrity of Worship* (Nashville: Abingdon Press, 1971).

[13] James F. White, *New Forms of Worship* (Nashville: Abingdon Press, 1971).

be especially helpful in seeking rationale for new forms of liturgy. It will help them answer the questions: "What is worship?" and "Why is it important to the Christian life?" It is a practical book which provides suggestions to inspire people's imagination.

Briefer essays on worship and the marriage service will be found in the *Companion to the Book of Worship*[14] of The United Methodist Church, parts of which were written by both White and Hoon. Chapter V, "The Order for the Service of Marriage," by Hoon treats the historical, pastoral, theological, and liturgical aspects of the marriage service.

Those who wish to create an experimental wedding service will find John Killinger's *Leave It to the Spirit*[15] an extremely helpful book. Concerned with commitment and freedom in the new liturgy, it seeks to relate church worship to our period style. Killinger advocates that worship be structured to evoke the fullest response from the participants. An

[14] William F. Dunkle, Jr., and Joseph D. Quillian, Jr. (ed.), *Companion to the Book of Worship* (Nashville: Abingdon Press, 1970).

[15] John Killinger, *Leave It to the Spirit* (New York: Harper & Row, 1971).

experimental wedding service so constructed
would contrast sharply with the usual wedding
performance where guests are spectators only.

The pamphlet "Planning the Wedding Service" [16] is a very helpful aid to planning a
wedding as an act of Christian worship. Another helpful resource is the May, 1972, issue
of *Liturgy*[17] which is a special issue on
weddings, with emphasis on the freewheeling
wedding celebration. Unfortunately this issue
is no longer available from the publisher. But
copies may be borrowed from public or church
libraries. Another booklet, "Celebrating the
Christian Marriage," [18] is an extremely valuable guide for the couple creating an experimental wedding service. It not only provides
resources but seeks to evoke from the couple
what they want to express in their wedding
celebration. By using their creativity a couple
can design a marriage festival that is fully

[16] Carl F. Schalk, "Planning the Wedding Service"
(order from: Concordia Publishing House, 3558 S. Jefferson Ave., Saint Louis, Mo. 63118).

[17] *Liturgy* 17 (May 1972), published by The Liturgical Conference, 1330 Massachusetts Ave., NW, Washington, D.C. 20005.

[18] "Creating the Christian Marriage" published by
Sacred Design, 840 Colorado Ave., So., Minneapolis,
Minn. 55416.

representative of their combined individuality. This booklet shows a couple how to make it happen.

Couples planning a free-wheeling marriage festival will find Nick Hodsdon's *The Joyful Wedding*[19] filled with helpful suggestions and folk music suited for weddings. It concentrates heavily on the music aspect of the wedding and offers basic guidance for writing a liturgy. No one would want to turn the wedding into a folk music festival, however. This can be avoided with firm guidance and tact.

Two books on worship as celebration which will assist couples in understanding the nature of celebration and how to plan for it are: *Contemporary Celebration*[20] by Ross Snyder and *Let it Happen*[21] by Reid and Kerns. They will also be helpful for the minister and church worship committee in designing services.

The New Wedding[22] by Khoren Arisian

[19] Nick Hodsdon, *The Joyful Wedding* (Nashville: Abingdon Press, 1973).

[20] Ross Snyder, *Contemporary Celebration* (Nashville: Abingdon Press, 1971).

[21] Clyde Reid and Jerry Kerns, *Let It Happen* (New York: Harper & Row, 1973).

[22] Khoren Arisian, *The New Wedding* (New York: Random House, 1973).

contains many brief wedding ceremonies, each with a particular emphasis reflecting the individuality of the couple being married. Written by a leader in the ethical culture movement, these services would need to be carefully evaluated and adapted for use in a Christian wedding. However, it gives good examples of what some couples have done and contains poetry, readings, and other resources which can be used in a wedding.

A book which evolved out of a request by a rabbi's son and his future wife for a personalized marriage service is *Write Your Own Wedding*.[23] The book lists the essential elements of the Jewish, Roman Catholic, and Protestant wedding services, gives examples, and offers a collection of resources for couples. It would be an extremely helpful aid for the minister and couple to use in planning an experimental wedding service.

A very useful tool for the couple planning a wedding of any kind is *Your Wedding Workbook*.[24] It contains a check list for the couple

[23] Mordecai L. Brill; Marlene Halpin; and William Genne, *Write Your Own Wedding* (New York: Association Press, 1973).
[24] Natalia Belting and James R. Hine, *Your Wedding*

to use in planning their wedding. Another resource for both couple and minister is a cassette by Dennis C. Benson entitled "The Wedding—An Enabling Process Tape for Planning the Event." [25]

There are many resources for poetry, music, and readings appropriate for Christian experimental wedding services. Criteria for evaluating such resources should be discussed by the minister and couple. Does the poem or reading reflect a Christian understanding of love and marriage or a secular one? Is it appropriate for a service of Christian worship? Does it exalt Christ? Collections of contemporary as well as classical poetry can be found in the public library, where one can carefully select materials. Or members of the wedding party may wish to compose a poem or song as a gift to the couple. William Flanders has written some folk songs specifically for weddings: "Rebekah's Song," "While We Have Time," and "You Have Made Me Trust You." [26] A

Workbook (order from The Interstate Printers, 19 Jackson St., Danville, Ill. 61832).

[25] Dennis C. Benson, "The Wedding" (Nashville: Abingdon Press, 1973).

[26] Available from William Flanders, 3714 Harrison St., NW, Washington, D.C. 20015.

recent collection of songs entitled *Folk Songs for Weddings*[27] contains a variety of new and old folk songs appropriate especially for a free-wheeling service.

Any wedding service will be enhanced by a wedding service bulletin. But in the free-wheeling service *a bulletin is a necessity* if the congregation and the wedding party are to follow the service and participate unless it is completely spontaneous. The bulletin will contain the words to any songs, responses, litanies, and prayers the congregation is expected to join in. It may also contain the couple's vows, names of members of the wedding party, new address and phone number of the couple, and names of clergy officiating. Everything needed for participation in the wedding service should be on *one* bulletin and should be simple to follow.

The Process Outlined

In the minister's first interview with the couple who wish to personalize their wedding service, he should ask them how they arrived

---

[27] *Folk Songs for Weddings* (Carol Stream, Ill.: Hope Publishing Co., 1972).

at the decision to write some or all of their service. The minister will usually ask what they have seen at other weddings which they liked or disliked. And he may want to assure them that at this point everything is negotiable.

The minister should have on hand copies of various styles of wedding liturgies including classical, contemporary, and free. He may ask to see copies of services they already have and like. Two issues of *The Christian Ministry*[28] magazine contain copies of wedding services and other resources for weddings. Copies of these and other examples of wedding services may be shared and discussed with the couple.

It may seem paradoxical, but couples who write their own vows are usually more conservative in their concept of marriage than many who do not. Original vows in the bride or groom's own words usually reflect a deeper and more personal commitment than do vows that are merely repeated. The very fact that the couple wishes to "buy into" the forming

[28] "New Liturgies: Order for The Celebration of Marriage," *The Christian Ministry* 1 (Nov., 1971), 14-17, and "The Practicum: Contemporary Wedding Ceremonies," *The Christian Ministry* 1 (May, 1970), 24-32.

of the service with their personal choices indicates a greater concern for making the wedding meaningful.

Choice heightens awareness. Thus the process of decision-making in creating all or part of a wedding service raises the level of consciousness of the persons involved.

After a number of premarriage interviews with the couple the minister will be able to help them decide when they are ready to select a unifying theme for their wedding service. And at this point they should be prepared to write out a rough draft of the vows they will make to each other. One couple went into separate rooms to do this. They did not reveal to the other what they had written until saying their vows in the service.

The vows are the *heart* of the wedding ceremony. In fact, the betrothal can be omitted along with one or both ring ceremonies. Or the ring ceremony can be combined with the vows so that the couple place the ring on each other's fingers while making their vows. The vows may be read by the minister with the couple affirming "I do" or "I will." But it is preferable if they will say the vows to each other. They may memorize

them, read them from the wedding bulletin
or a card, or be prompted by the minister.

*The marriage covenant is made by the bride
and groom joining right hands and saying
their vows.* Vows should reflect a lifelong
commitment which recognizes the negative as
well as positive aspects of life. The mature
love and fidelity pledged should squarely face
sickness, disappointment, and failure, which
are inevitable in life. Some include a commitment to work together for social justice and
world peace, recognizing their responsibility
not only to each other but to society. And
some pledge to love and support the children
they may have in the future.

After the vows are written, the wedding
ceremony is shaped around them. The selection of music, prayers, scripture, poetry,
litanies, etc., should reflect the theme of the
wedding expressed in the vows.

When a rough draft of the entire wedding
ceremony is completed the couple should be
asked if their parents are "in" or "out" of
their wedding plans if this has not already been
determined. If they are "in," then a copy of
the rough draft should be sent to parents.
Some may want to ask for comments. This

approach allows parents to participate in the wedding service, especially an unconventional one. If the bride's mother knows ahead of time that the traditional wedding processional will not be used she will not be shocked at the wedding, although she may not be happy with the substitute.

The wedding should serve to *strengthen*, not weaken, family ties. In fact, the couple may want to dramatize the uniting of their two families by inviting both sets of parents to join them in the chancel when the bride arrives there. The parents may give the bride and groom to each other and join hands for a moment as a new, larger family. A parent or parents may make a brief statement recognizing the bride and groom as adults and welcoming the new son and daughter into the family.

The wedding is a rite of passage, the sign of persons moving from one way of life to another. No one moves easily from one form of life to another. A time of affirmation of family ties during the event can make the rite of passage easier for all involved. Gestures and words can make this rite of passage even more meaningful.

The pronouncement of the couple as husband and wife and the giving of the blessing on their marriage will be done, of course, by the minister. But the couple may wish to discuss it and offer suggestions. With the pronouncement of the couple as husband and wife some ministers address them with words of admonition and counsel before giving the blessing. One minister whispers the words of counsel to the couple only and gives them a verse of scripture to guide them in their new relationship.

Another gesture which has become popular is a candle-lighting ceremony by bride and groom. This can effectively dramatize the meaning of this rite of passage. There are several ways it may be done.

The bride and groom, each carrying a taper, move to the ends of the altar. Each lights his or her taper from a large candle there, blows out the candle, and moves to the center of the altar. There the bride and groom light a single large candle.

If this seems to ring too much of marriage-as-disappearance-of-self, the couple together may light the two altar candles after the vows. The candles may be their gift to the church, or the church's gift to them. The candles serve as reminders of Christ, the Light of the World, who blesses Christian marriage and who said, "The two shall be one flesh." As the couple go through the actions of lighting candles the minister may wish to read appropriate passages of scripture and interpret their actions for the congregation.

The kiss of peace is another gesture which is being used in wedding services. An ancient Christian ritual of Christian brotherhood, this ritual is usually performed by a double hand-clasp and words like these, "Peace be with you, Jan." And the reply is, "And with your spirit, George." Bride and groom may pass the peace to members of the congregation after their vows, or at the conclusion of the service. It is especially appropriate at the conclusion of Communion climaxing a wedding service.

You, the minister, have been asked by the couple to help them make their wedding service the most meaningful event of their lives. They look to you for guidance, counsel, and support. And they are counting on you to see that what you three have planned together *happens* in their wedding service.

CONDUCTING THE SERVICE

The Christian wedding, whether celebrated privately in a home or publicly in church, should be planned and conducted as a service of worship and not a performance. Christ, not the bride or couple, should be the focus of the Christian wedding. Those who elect to have a Christian ceremony rather than a civil wedding service should expect to be guided by the Scriptures and church traditions rather than by current fads.

Before conducting a wedding service a minister should become informed regarding marriage laws of the particular state in which the wedding is to take place. Some states require the minister to be bonded. Others require a certain waiting period. In some states laws vary by the counties of the state. He should make certain that the marriage license was issued in the county in which the wedding is to take place when this is required.

In performing a wedding ceremony in the United States a minister acts as both a religious celebrant and a civil representative of the state. He is not required by law to marry any couple. But when he consents to perform a service of marriage he is obligated to fill in properly the license and sign and return it to the civil authority of the county in which the marriage is performed.

The completed wedding license should be returned promptly by mail or in person to the proper civil authority.

The wedding rehearsal and ceremony is under the *sole direction* of the minister. The directory for worship of one denomination states unequivocally: "The Christian marriage service is a service of worship before God . . . and the service shall be under the sole direction of the minister." In the interview to plan the wedding service the minister should inform the bride if he wishes the assistance of a florist or bridal consultant in conducting the rehearsal and wedding. If he does not, he should make this clear to the bride so that there will be no misunderstanding at the rehearsal or wedding.

While many bridal consultants can offer valuable assistance in positioning the bridal party in the chancel and in starting the members of the processional at the proper time, this function can also be performed by an experienced member of the church's altar guild or worship committee. If the minister chooses to accept the assistance of a bridal consultant he should make it clear to the consultant before the rehearsal the function he is to perform.

The wedding policy statement of one church says, in regard to rehearsals: "The rector and church organist will always direct the rehearsal. They will welcome suggestions, but their word will be the final one. *No professional bridal consultant will be present at the rehearsal.* The rector and organist have found from experience that the rehearsal and the wedding will go more smoothly if no professional bridal consultant is present. A member of the Altar Guild will be present at both the rehearsal and the wedding to help the wedding party. *The bride should expect to take the part of the bride in the rehearsal.*" Another church's policy states that all requests for type of service and changes in service, including positioning of the bridal party, must be made in consultation with the minister prior to the time of the rehearsal.

If the minister chooses to direct the rehearsal and wedding without assistance from a bridal consultant or florist, he should meet with the bride in the place where the wedding will be held ahead of time and make notes regarding her preferences in conducting the processional, ceremony, and recessional. *This is essential if the rehearsal is to go smoothly.* There is nothing more frustrating than attempting to conduct a large rehearsal with too many directors. One bridal consultant indicated she preferred leaving the entire direction of the rehearsal to the minister but that she knew of only three ministers who could direct one smoothly. She emphasized the necessity of prior planning with the bride so that the minister can give clear instructions to each person in the wedding party.

During the planning of the rehearsal the minister should ask if there are special problems regarding seating of parents of the bride or groom when any of them have been divorced. A book on wedding etiquette and common sense can enable the bride and minister to plan seating so that unpleasant situations can be avoided. This applies also to the receiving line at the reception.

The minister functions in the wedding as director, prompter, and participant. As director he will find it helpful to have the advice of a recent book on wedding etiquette as well as his own denomination's worshipbook. One such book, an inexpensive paperback, is *Weddings* by Rosalie Brody.[1] Other general books on social etiquette have chapters on wedding etiquette.

Flexibility and creativity characterize weddings today more so than in the past. The desire of a couple to personalize their wedding service need not be cause for resistance or alarm on the part of either family or the minister.

The Rehearsal

The rehearsal of the wedding ceremony has become a standard procedure for weddings other than small, private affairs. The rehearsal is usually held the day before or two days before the wedding. Late afternoon *before* the rehearsal dinner is the most popular time. Conducting the rehearsal first allows for a leisurely

[1] Rosalie Brody, *Weddings* (New York: Simon & Schuster, Inc., 1963).

rehearsal dinner. Otherwise the dinner party
may be rushed.

If begun on time and there are no hitches,
the rehearsal should take no longer than thirty
to forty-five minutes.

The rehearsal should be held in the place
where the wedding will take place. All members of the wedding party, including the bride,
should rehearse. In his last interview with the
couple the minister should ask them to urge
all members of the wedding party to arrive on
time for the rehearsal. The organist should be
on hand to rehearse. Soloists and other musicians may rehearse with the organist at another
time. This is preferred since it shortens the
time required for the rehearsal.

The rehearsal begins when the minister asks
all members of the wedding party to sit in the
front pews. He may want to welcome those
who are not members of the congregation. In
order to set the tone of the rehearsal he may
want to say something like this:

We are gathered here to rehearse the wedding service of our friends Jan and George. If each of us
will listen carefully to instructions and learn our
parts well then we will be comfortable in our

roles during the wedding. We will rehearse the service as many times as necessary for you to be certain of your part. Usually thirty to forty-five minutes is sufficient. Please feel free to ask questions you may have.

Let us bow our heads for prayer as we ask God's guidance and blessing:

> Gracious God, thank you for allowing us to share Jan's and George's happiness as they prepare to be married. Guide us that we may contribute our best to you and to them in the ceremony. May the Spirit of the Living Christ infect us with joy as we now prepare for the celebration of their marriage. Bless us we humbly pray. Amen.

This or a similar introduction and prayer can help create an atmosphere of cooperation and joyful dignity for the rehearsal and wedding.

Unfortunately there is a temptation on the part of some members of wedding parties to clown around during the rehearsal. This not only wastes time but detracts from the purpose of the rehearsal. The minister should encourage concentration here.

After the opening prayer the minister may want to give a brief overview of the rehearsal like this:

The wedding ceremony is a worship service in the Christian tradition. God has ordained marriage and Jesus blessed marriage by his presence at the wedding at Cana. As we rehearse we may think of the wedding as a little drama consisting of three acts. Act I is the processional. Act II is the ceremony itself, and act III is the recessional. Contrary to the usual practice in rehearsing a drama, the wedding is best rehearsed by beginning with act III! Then we move to act I, the processional, and then acts II and III. Let us begin by taking our proper places in the chancel. First, will Jan and George please come take their places, with George on my left and Jan on my right. Next, will Jan's maid of honor take her place on Jan's left? And now will the best man take his place on George's right? The bridesmaids will please come forward and take their places to my right and the ushers will take their places to my left. (If there is a ring bearer and flower girl they should be seated with their parents after the processional rather than stand during the ceremony. The father of the bride will also have been seated earlier in the service.)

Now the bridesmaids and ushers should be positioned. Their positions should have been planned earlier by the minister and bride and sketched out with the names of each written in. They may be arranged in ascending or descending order of height from the bride or alternating tall and short. They need not be in a straight line but may alternate being forward and behind or may be in an arc. The arrangement of the chancel, number in the wedding party, and preference of the bride will determine the arrangement. It may be necessary to make some minor changes at the rehearsal in order to achieve the desired arrangement. The diagrams on pages 66 and 67 illustrate two possible arrangements. One is for a church with a central aisle and the other is for a church with a double aisle.

If the bride, maid of honor, groom, best man, and minister(s) are to advance farther toward the altar after the bride has been given by her father this final position should now be taken. It is from this position that the recessional will begin. Each person should be asked to observe carefully where he/she is standing. During the rehearsal it may be helpful to place a hymnbook or other object on the floor to mark the places for each bridesmaid and usher. By the end of the rehearsal they should have learned their positions in relation to the chan-

Church With Center Aisle

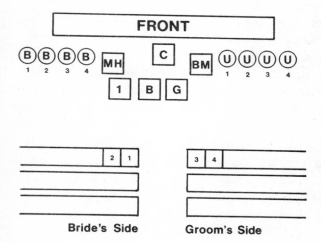

1-Bride's Father
2-Bride's Mother
3-Groom's Father
4-Groom Mother

C- Clergyman
G- Groom
B- Bride

MH- Maid of Honor
BM- Best Man
U_1- Ushers -(1, 2, 3, 4)
B_1- Bridesmaids -(1, 2, 3, 4)

Church Without Center Aisle

(ALTERNATE ARRANGEMENTS OF ATTENDANTS)

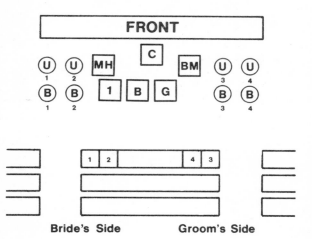

1 - Bride's Father
2 - Bride's Mother
3 - Groom's Father
4 - Groom Mother

C - Clergyman
G - Groom
B - Bride

MH - Maid of Honor
BM - Best Man
U_1 - Ushers - [1, 2, 3, 4]
B_1 - Bridesmaids - [1, 2, 3, 4]

cel furniture and each other so that it will not
need to be marked.

The minister now signals to the organist to
begin the recessional music. The entire wedding party recesses to the rear of the church.
The order for the recessional is as follows:
bride and groom, ring bearer and flower girl
(unless they have been seated with parents,
which is desirable), maid of honor (either
alone or on arm of best man or an usher). In
an ultra formal wedding the best man follows
the minister to the minister's study to give him
the fee entrusted to him by the groom. It is optional whether the bridesmaids recess alone or
on arms of ushers. They are followed by ushers
if the ushers do not escort the bridesmaids.
Any ushers not escorting bridesmaids recess in
pairs. In large weddings when the bridesmaids
have processed in pairs they may also recess
in pairs, followed by the ushers in pairs.

When the ceremony is climaxed by a celebration of the Lord's Supper, the wedding
party may be seated on the front pews or special chairs during the sacrament; or they may
choose to remain standing as the size of the
congregation and circumstances indicate a
preferred position. Also, if there is a lengthy

homily the wedding party may be seated for this.

In some weddings the bride and groom wish to be present for the wedding music. In this case the wedding party would not process in but would informally take their places in the front pew or in chairs in the chancel area. The form of the wedding service will determine the preferable arrangement and procedure.

The processional is now practiced. The groom and best man go to the door through which they will enter with the minister. The bride, bride's father, and other members of the bridal party take their places at the rear of the church. Someone will be needed to start them at the right time. A friend of the family, bridal consultant, member of the altar guild, etc., may do this. This person should be given a list of the persons in the order in which they are to process. He signals to the organist to begin the processional. The minister, groom, and best man, in that order, come in and take their places at the head of the aisle. There they await the rest of the bridal party. As the minister takes his place the ushers enter. They may come either from the same entrance used by the minister or from the rear of the sanctuary.

Where there are two aisles the ushers may enter by one and the bridesmaids by the other. The ushers may enter by twos or may escort a bridesmaid. When the ushers reach their positions at the chancel they face toward the center aisle. They stand with their hands either at their sides or folded in front with left over right or with hands behind them. But all ushers should follow the same pattern. They should feel free to smile pleasantly as the other members of the bridal party process.

The bridesmaids enter next, spaced about fifteen feet apart for a long aisle, ten to twelve feet for a short aisle. In a large wedding they may enter in pairs. They are followed by the maid of honor, ring bearer and flower girl. The flower girl is *always* the last to process before the bride.

The bride and her father enter next with her father on her left. They pause for a moment at the head of the center aisle so that the "starter" can straighten her train. The organist signals the entrance of the bride with a joyous crescendo. The bride and her father begin on their left foot and process, keeping in step. It is optional for the congregation to stand for the processional.

The bride on the arm of her father (or male relative) proceeds to the center of the aisle and stops in front of the minister, about two feet away. The organ fades out promptly.

The minister may then read through all or key parts of the wedding service. He will find it helpful if previously he has written the name of the bride and groom which they wish to use in the vows on a slip of paper and secured it with a paper clip in the servicebook. (In some areas middle names are very important.)

The minister's question of the bride's father, "Who gives this woman to be wed?" is the signal for the bride to release her father's arm and transfer her bouquet from her right to left hand. The bride's father may answer the question by either silently, or with the words "I do" or "Her mother and I do" placing the bride's right hand in the right hand of the minister. The bride's father is then seated by the bride's mother and next to the aisle. If the congregation has been standing for the processional, they may be seated at this point.

The minister then places the bride's right hand in the groom's right hand. Bride and groom face each other as they say their vows. If the vows are to be said farther up toward the altar the minister, bride, groom, maid of honor, and best man move to their new positions immediately after the minister places the bride's hand in the groom's. They may need to drop hands in order to move to the new position. The bride may steady herself on the arm of the groom as they move.

In rehearsing the vows in a large sanctuary it is well to leave someone in the rear to listen to see if the vows can be heard. If not, the bride and groom should raise the level of their voices. As the bride and groom say their vows to each other they should look into each other's eyes while making this solemn covenant. After the groom says his vow to the bride the couple loose right hands. Then the bride takes the groom's right hand in hers as she says her vow to him.

Then the bride gives her flowers to her maid of honor for the ring ceremony. The best man will either already have the ring for the bride before the service began or he will have received it from the ring bearer at the end of the processional. The maid of honor, if there is a double ring ceremony, holds the ring for the groom. The rings can be carried safely on one of the attendants' fingers until needed in the service. If a ring is accidentally dropped the best man should rescue it. If the bride wears gloves she should either remove the glove or the third finger of the left glove should be cut beforehand. The bride wears her engagement ring on her right hand for the service but after the service places it on her left hand over the wedding band.

The best man gives the ring to the minister who offers a prayer of blessing and then gives it to the groom. As the groom places it on the third finger of the bride's left hand he says the ring vow. Next the maid of honor gives the groom's ring to the minister who offers a prayer of blessing and gives it to the bride. (This transfer of rings is easily done if the ring is placed in the palm of the minister's hand and taken from his palm.) The bride places the ring on the groom's third finger of his left hand as she says the ring vow.

When there is a prayer bench the couple kneels for prayer. Otherwise they remain standing as the minister offers a prayer followed by the Lord's Prayer prayed by everyone. (Many ministers feel that the Lord's Prayer should be the first prayer said together by the new husband and wife and the congregation and should *not* be sung as a solo.)

The couple then stands and the minister declares them husband and wife. The minister asks them to again join right hands and he says, "Whom God has joined together . . ."

The minister pronounces the benediction. (They may choose to kneel for the benediction if they did not kneel for the earlier prayer and Lord's Prayer.) If kneeling for prayer, they now stand.

Next the bride's veil is lifted by either the maid of honor or the groom. When the bride's father or close relative has performed the ceremony and may wish to kiss the bride the groom kisses her at this point in the ceremony. Otherwise, the kiss is properly reserved for later at the rear of the church.

The maid of honor gives the bride her bouquet and helps straighten her train before the bride takes her husband's arm and they recess to the rear of the church. The organist begins the recessional music when the bride and groom are ready to recess. She takes the groom's right arm as they go out the center aisle. The recessional continues as rehearsed earlier.

The processional should now be repeated. Check with the organist to see if he is comfortable with the procedure and timing. Ask members of the wedding party if they have any questions. Then ask if they are comfortable with their roles. If everyone is satisfied with the rehearsal to this point the organist may be excused to practice with the soloist or to leave.

With the wedding party in place any or all of the ceremony may be practiced as it is felt necessary. The bride and groom should practice clasping their right hands as they face each other to exchange vows. Emphasize the eye to eye contact as they make this solemn covenant before God and witnesses.

The exchange of rings should be practiced until it can be done with ease. In the rehearsal and wedding the minister may want to comment on the meaning of this gesture. It reflects older symbolic exchanges of property and the endowing of each other with all one's worldly goods. (Although the older phrases "with all my worldly goods I thee endow" and "with my body I thee worship" have been dropped from most wedding liturgies some couples may wish to reintroduce them.) The ring, made of precious metal, symbolizes the purity of the love they are to share with each other. The circular shape of the ring which has no end symbolizes their love which they pledge to each other "until death do us part."

If the bride and groom choose to kneel for prayer this also should be practiced. The maid of honor should be coached to take care of the bride's dress and train so that she can rise without difficulty. The bride may want to practice giving her bouquet to her maid of honor and receiving it again. And the maid of honor may want to practice lifting the veil and straightening the train.

Then reassemble the wedding party in the front pews. Let the ushers practice their roles by seating bridesmaids as if they were guests. The ushers should be instructed to ask guests if they are relatives of the bride or groom. The bride's relatives are seated on the left side of the church and the groom's relatives on the right side within spaces reserved by ribbons. If guests are not relatives of the bride or groom ushers should attempt to seat them so that the sanctuary is balanced with about as many guests on one side as the other. Ushers may need to be shown how to extend their right arm for ladies to hold as they are led to a seat, while their husbands and children follow. The ushers who are to seat the bride's mother and groom's mother and any grandmothers should be assigned, and this may be practiced. The grandmothers are seated, then the groom's mother. The bride's mother is seated last. Then the aisle runner is unrolled.

The ushers who are to light the candles should practice this procedure. They should make sure they know where the tapers are located and should be reminded to extinguish the candles as soon as the pictures are made after the ceremony. They should also be cautioned to make sure each candle is lighted well and to work in unison. They begin from the outside of the candelabra and work to the center.

The usual procedure for the wedding service is as follows:

1. prelude music (timed by the organist so that the bride can process on the hour announced for the wedding)
2. seating of guests by ushers
3. candles lighted
4. groom's parents are seated
5. bride's mother is seated

6. aisle runner is laid
7. vocal or other music
8. wedding processional
9. the marriage ceremony
10. the recessional
11. bride's parents are ushered out followed by groom's parents and grandparents
12. congregation is dismissed

The person who serves as the "starter" for the wedding will need to alert the ushers when to light the candles, seat mothers, lay runner, and usher out parents.

Before dismissing the rehearsal make certain everyone knows the place and time he/she is to appear for the wedding. Ushers normally arrive an hour before the service begins.

The groom should give the minister the marriage license at the rehearsal. The minister should review it to make sure it is in order. If witnesess are required the minister should alert the best man and maid of honor to sign it after the wedding. If the state does not provide the couple with a marriage certificate the minister may want to have a supply of such certificates on hand. They can be purchased from church supply houses. It should be filled in, signed, and given to the couple before they leave on the honeymoon.

The Double Wedding

The double wedding is similar to the single except for the following differences. The two bridegrooms follow the minister and stand, side by side, each with his best man behind him. The groom of the older sister should be nearer the aisle. Ushers of both bridegrooms go up the aisle together. The bridesmaids of the older sister, followed by her maid of honor enter next. The older sister follows on the right arm of her father. Next in order come the bridesmaids of the younger sister, her maid of honor, and last the younger sister on the arm of a brother, uncle, or nearest relative.

When There Are Two or More Ministers

The bride's own pastor should be asked to perform the wedding unless her father or a close relative of the couple is a clergyman. In which case the bride asks her pastor to invite the relative to conduct the service and invites her pastor to assist. Other ministers may be asked to assist the bride's pastor in the church he serves, and the invitation should be extended through him. The two ministers confer and divide the wedding ceremony leadership between them. Usually the assisting minister leads the first part of the service through the question to the bride's father. Then the minister in charge takes the service from this point on. The assisting minister may lead the Lord's Prayer and give the benediction. When there are additional ministers the leadership of the service may be similarly shared.

Wedding of a Clergyman's Daughter

When the bride's father is a clergyman she may ask him to perform the ceremony and give her away also. Or she may ask a brother or other male relative to give her away. But if she wishes to have her father give her away and perform the service she may ask another clergyman to conduct the first part of the service through the question to the bride's father. After giving his daughter in marriage the minister then moves to a new position from which he conducts the remainder of the service.

If the bride's mother is a minister and is asked to perform the ceremony this is done in the usual fashion. Here the seating of the groom's mother is the signal for the processional to begin. The bride's father gives her away and takes a seat in the front pew.

Variations

Every wedding is different because of personal preferences. One couple chose to hear the music at their wedding. They entered from separate places and sat together with their wedding party in the front of the church. Then they took their places for the ceremony. When the wedding ceremony follows a regular congregational service of worship, which is becoming more frequent, the couple and their attendants may take their places for the ceremony without processing. Other variations are discussed in the chapter "Making the Wedding More Personal."

The Home or Garden Wedding

The same procedure is followed for the processional as in the church wedding. In the home wedding the wedding party proceeds down the stairs to the place where the service is to be performed. In a garden wedding they proceed from the house to the place where the ceremony is to be conducted. A prayer bench may be rented or borrowed if desired. In small private home weddings the processional is eliminated.

After the ceremony there is no recessional. When the minister withdraws at the conclusion of the service the bride and groom merely turn to receive congratulations from their guests. When there is no recessional the groom always kisses his bride before they turn to receive their guests.

The Marriage Ceremony
in the Minister's Home or Study

The bride and groom usually come to the minister's home or study together and are met there by their families and a few invited friends. The minister reads the service and the couple are congratulated afterwards by family and friends. They then proceed to the place for the reception.

The Blessing of a Civil Marriage

This service is conducted similarly to the regular service except that at the beginning of the service it is announced that they have already been married by the law of the state.

The Wedding as Part of a
Regular Worship Service

It is becoming more common for couples to be married at the end of a regular congregational worship service. There is good church tradition to support this practice which is rather common in the Church of Scotland.

MUSIC AND THE WEDDING

In most churches the minister will refer the bride and groom to the church organist to help them select appropriate music for their wedding. A well-trained musician with a biblical foundation and an understanding of the place of music in the church's life can be a real asset to the couple. But the minister can also give them some guidance in their choice of music.

Problems regarding the choice of music for weddings arise usually with couples coming from the fringe of the church's life. Persons nurtured in the church have a greater concern that the music for their wedding reflect a Christian understanding of marriage. But those on the fringe may ask for music of a thoroughly secular nature. Music from Broadway hits or popular movies is, unfortunately, used in some weddings today.

In guiding the couple in the choice of wedding music the minister may want to raise the basic question: "Why have a church wedding?" This question naturally leads to the next one: "What do I do to express the reason I have come to church to be married?" The minister can ask these questions without judging the couple and their motives.

Music speaks for its age and reflects its age. Couples considering particular pieces of music should be encouraged to ask: "Is this music raising up the life-style and values which I want to emphasize?" Each couple has to reach their own answer. But they should do it with integrity.

The church wedding service is the church at worship and the church in witness. Music in the wedding should contribute to Christian worship and witness. Some people come to weddings who seldom, if ever, attend regular church services. The entire wedding service, but especially the choice and performance of the music, can be a credit to the church's worship and witness.

Music which is associated with certain words is easier to evaluate than music which has no words. The latter can only be judged on the symbolic level. This can be tricky for the layman, and a trained musician is needed to guide the couple. But when there are words associated with the music, the words should be judged on the basis of their appropriateness for a service of Christian worship.

Most ministers feel (and I feel emphatically) that the words to music used in a church wedding should not be humanistic or Gnostic. Gnostic music says that the world has a problem, but if we just love a little more we can, by our own efforts, make the world better. Humansitic music has no transcendental reference. Human love, but especially romantic love, is all we need for success in marriage. Neither Gnostic nor humanistic songs lead to deeper faith in God and reliance upon him for love, forgiveness, and life.

Many churches have allowed secular music to become associated with church weddings. "Because," "I Love You Truly," "O Promise Me," "One Hand, One Heart," "The Impossible Dream," "Through the Years," and "One Alone," are among the best-known non-religious songs for Christian weddings. Most ministers also feel (and I am in full agreement) that traditional wedding marches are inappropriate and were never intended for use in a religious ceremony.

The "Bridal Chorus" from Wagner's *Lohengrin* is associated with the parody "Here comes the bride." It occurs in the opera after the wedding in an atmosphere of distrust and hatred concluded by death and separation. Mendelssohn's recessional march from *Incidental Music* written for *A Midsummer Night's Dream* by Shakespeare was played before Act IV in which Bottom, the weaver, is turned into an ass with all the clowning and foolishness he produced. Both pieces were originally written for full orchestra and not for the organ.

Since the chief reason for having a church wedding rather than a civil one is to acknowledge the Christian significance of marriage it follows that any music used in a church wedding should be worthy of the worship of Almighty God. Instrumental music should evoke the spirit of prayer or praise. Any vocal texts should be God-centered and not man-centered. Such music expresses the joyful gratitude of the couple and guests for God's gift of love. It also conveys a sense of reverence for the sacred relationship into which the bride and groom have been called.

The music selected for the wedding service should not be considered a "cover" for the seating of guests or entertainment before the main event. Rather, it should set the mood of worship. The vocalist, if used, should point up the religious significance of this great step in the lives of the bride and groom.

The church wedding, in contrast to the civil marriage service, is an occasion of *corporate* worship. The service should be one of *participation,* not of observation. The bride and groom should be encouraged to involve the congregation in worship through the use of hymns, responses, and corporate prayers. The Lord's Prayer should be prayed by the congregation and wedding party and not sung as a solo.

There is a trend away from vocal soloists in church weddings. The minister of music of a large metropolitan church reports that in a recent summer vocalists were used in only two out of fifteen church weddings for which he played. In other recent summers no vocalists were used. However, choirs are being used to lead congregational singing and for special music.

The preceremony music need not be limited to the organ or piano. The harp, harpsicord, flute, violin, bell choir, trombone, clarinet, flute, trumpet, guitar, and chamber music ensembles are being used effectively in church weddings. The music chosen should be selected for the contribution it will make to the total worship service. Many brides want only soft music in order to create a kind of romantic atmosphere which sometimes borders on the funereal.

Preceremony music should consist of contrasts—meditative interspersed with sprightly, louder music. Music selected may represent many periods. The bride and groom should allow the musician some leeway in selecting the music with which he feels comfortable and which is suitable for the particular instrument.[1] The European custom of leaving the selection of wedding music entirely to the decision of the musician would be desirable in many instances. The training and musical insight of the church organist should guide the

[1] See p. 91 ff.

couple rather than current fads and their pre-conceived ideas of what wedding music consists.

The bride and groom often have some particular song which has become "their" song during courtship. Frequently the bride wants "their song" played at the wedding. But unless it can pass the test of music fitting for a Christian worship service it should be reserved for a social gathering such as a reception or dinner party. Sentimental love songs or semi-classics can add to the enjoyment of a re-hearsal dinner. But they do *not* belong in a service of Christian worship.

One church publishes a wedding brochure to guide couples and in it sets forth the following policy regarding wedding music:

Because the ceremony is set in the context of worship, the music used in the wedding is ex-pected to be religious. This automatically elimi-nates certain vocal numbers which are used in some weddings. As an aid to the bride the follow-ing music is suggested for consideration. If some number is desired which is not listed here, the request may be submitted to the Session's Com-mittee on Worship through the minister.

The music listed does not, of course, include the traditional wedding Wagner processional and Mendelssohn recessional. The brochure encourages the use of a wedding bulletin and congregational participation in hymns, responsive readings, and prayers.

An extremely helpful cassette designed to assist the couple in selecting appropriate wedding music can be played on either a stereo or monaural player. It is available from Parrigin and Shaw, Presbyterian Student Center, 100 Hitt St., Columbia, Mo. 65201. One side of the cassette features samples of organ music from Baroque, Romantic, and present-day composers. The other side is a recording of complete organ selections of preludes, processionals, and recessionals which may be amplified and used in a wedding when an organ is not available.

Other resources a church should have on hand to give to couples are as follows:

> Wedding Music by Fryxell, Fortress Press, 2900 Queen Lane, Philadelphia, Pa. 19129
> Music For Weddings, Abingdon Press, 201 Eighth Ave., S., Nashville, Tenn. 37202
> Planning a Christian Wedding, by Paul

Krause, Concordia Pub. Co., 3558 S. Jefferson Ave. St. Louis, Mo. 63118

Music for Church Weddings, The Seabury Press, Greenwich, Conn. 06830

Music and Your Wedding, by Linda and William Epley, available from Sunday School Board, Southern Baptist Convention, Nashville, Tenn.

Weddings in a Presbyterian Congregation, by Paul H. Richards, distributed by Division of National Mission, 341 Ponce de Leon Ave., NE, Atlanta, Ga. 30308

Wedding Music (2 Vols.), Concordia Publishing House, 3558 S. Jefferson Ave., St. Louis, Mo. 63118 (an invaluable source of wedding music for church musicians)

Folk Songs for Weddings, Hope Publishing Co., Carol Stream, Illinois, 60187 (Wide range of quality)

A few suggestions of music appropriate for a Christian wedding are as follows:

Processionals:

Processional on "Westminster Abbey" by R. Wetzler

Trumpet Tunes by Purcell

"Prince of Denmark's March" by Jeremiah Clark (commonly known as Trumpet Voluntary by Purcell)

Air (*Water Music*) by Handel

Chorale (*Suite Gothic*) by Boellmann

"Psalm XIX" by Marcello

Trumpet Tunes of Jeremiah Clark

Processional in G Major by Handel

Familiar church hymns such as the following may be used:

"Joyful, Joyful, We Adore Thee"—Tune: Hymn to Joy

"Love Divine, All Love Excelling"— Tune: Hyfrydol

"Praise to the Lord, the Almighty"— Tune: Lobe Den Herren

Recessionals

Trumpet Tunes by Purcell

Toccata (Symphony V) by Widor

Chorale (Suite Gothic) by Boellmann

Allegro (Symphony VI) by Vierne

"Psalm XIX" by Marcello

"In Thee Is Gladness" by Bach

"Now Thank We All Our God" by Karg-Elert

Chromatic Fugue by Pachelbel
Postlude in G by Handel
"Epithalame" (Sortie) by Healey Willan
Trumpet Voluntary by J. Stanley
Allegro Maestoso (*Water Music*) by Handel

In addition to the hymn "Now Thank We All Our God" other hymns may be used such as:

"O God, Our Help in Ages Past"—H. Fleischer
"The King of Love My Shepherd Is"—Tune: Dominus Regist Me
"Jesus, Thou Joy of Loving Hearts!"—Tune: Rimington

Preceremony Organ Recital

"Sheep and Lambs May Safely Graze" by Bach
"Jesu Joy of Man's Desiring" by Bach
"Brother James' Air" by Jacob (arr.)
"Lord Jesus Christ Be Present Now" by Walther
"Our Father, Thou in Heaven Above" by Schneider

*Adagio (Sonata in F Minor) by
  Mendelssohn
"Let All Together Praise Our God" by
  Bach
Adagio movements from organ sympho-
  nies of Widor, Vierne, etc.
Chorale Preludes in "Wedding Music"
  (Vol. II), published by Concordia
Benedictus by Reger
Choral by Jongen
*Variations on "A Mighty Fortress" by
  Cor Kee
Handel's Organ Concertos or Sonatas
Chorale Preludes based on appropriate
  hymns of praise
*Adagio from Oboe Concerto by Mar-
  cello, published by Concordia
* Aria by Flor Peeters, published by Edi-
  tion Heuwkemekjer, Amsterdam
*"Three Quiet Preludes" by Frederick
  Jacobi, published by H. W. Gray Co.
*Selections from the following collec-
  tions:
  Eight Slow Movements by Corelli,
  published by C. F. Peters
  Four Slow Movements From Sonatas

by Mendelssohn, published by Augsburg

Music for Worship (With Easy Pedals) by David Johnson

*Denotes easier organ selections

Suggested Vocal Music

"Entreat Me Not to Leave Thee" by Gounod

"O Father, All Creating" by Fetler

"Wedding Hymn" (*Ptolemy*) by Handel

"A Wedding Benediction" by Austin Lovelace

"O Perfect Love," the hymn by Barnby; or Leo Sowerby, published by H. W. Gray Co.

"Seal Us, O Holy Spirit," the hymn by Meredith

"O Lord Most Holy" by C. Franck

"Jesus Shepherd, Be Thou Near Me" by Bach

"O Love That Casts Out Fear" by Bach

"The Lord is My Shepherd" (Psalm 23), arrangements by many composers

"Jesu Joy of Man's Desiring" by Bach

"Thanks Be to Thee" by Handel

Also see Dvorak, *Biblical Songs, Book I,* published by Association Music, for selections such as "God Is My Shepherd," "I Will Sing New Songs of Gladness," and "Sing Ye a Joyful Song."

Suggested Hymns for Congregational Use

(processional, recessional, or in the service)

"Jesus, Thou Joy of Loving Hearts"—Tune: Rimington

"Joyful, Joyful We Adore Thee"—Tune: Hyfrydol

"Now Thank We All Our God"—Tune: Nun Danket

"O Perfect Love"—Tune: O Perfect Love

"Praise, My Soul, the King of Heaven"—Tune: Lauda Anima

"Praise to the Lord, the Almighty"—Tune: Lobe Den Herrn

"The King of Love My Shepherd Is"—Tune: Dominus Regist Me

As a Benediction: "May the Grace of Christ our Savior"—Tune: Sardis

GUIDELINES FOR WEDDINGS AND RECEPTIONS

A church which does not have a published official policy statement regarding weddings and receptions would do well to consider drawing up one. Such a policy statement can prevent misunderstandings and embarrassment when unusual requests are made. And it may relieve the minister, organist, or other individuals of the responsibility for making decisions forced on them by a crisis. It can be either mimeographed or printed in a booklet, and a copy should be given each bride and groom. Copies should also be available in the church library, office, and vestibule. A copy of a sample wedding and reception guide will be found on pp. 106-15.

The pastor is looked to for leadership in the development of policies regarding weddings since the wedding service is under his sole direction. Usually it is his expressed con-

cern which initiates a study of wedding procedures by the church's worship committee or
commission. The pastor and organist should
serve as advisory members of such a study
committee. The committee should study the
present practices of the church, policy statements of other churches, and other materials
concerned with weddings and receptions in
the church.

When the committee completes its study it
should submit it to the governing body of the
church for its consideration and adoption.
Such a report should be as detailed as the
particular needs of the local congregation require. It should reflect the church's view of
Christian marriage and a business approach
to the use of its staff personnel and facilities
for weddings and receptions.

One church located near a large university
found it helpful to require a written reservation request for the use of the church's
facilities for weddings and receptions. A
deposit, the amount to be determined by the
church administrator, is required at the time
the reservation is made. In small churches the
request is usually made through the church
secretary, and no deposit is required. The

governing body of some churches regularly grant permission for the use of church facilities for weddings and receptions.

Some churches charge a fee for the use of their facilities when neither bride nor groom nor their parents are members of the local congregation. Other churches charge a fee which pays for the additional custodial service required at weddings and receptions of members and nonmembers alike.

The custodian and other church employees should be paid for the additional work required for weddings and receptions. The policy statement should indicate either a set amount or an hourly wage for sexton, maid, church hostess, and any other employees.

The job description for the church organist should indicate whether or not he is expected to play for weddings as one of the duties for which he is paid a salary or whether he can expect to receive fees for such services rendered. If the church organist is to receive a fee for rehearsals and weddings, this should be indicated in the policy statement with the amount stated. Some churches stipulate that the church organist is to be paid the usual fee even though the bride may wish to invite a guest organist to play for her wedding.

When professional florists, caterers, and photographers who are not familiar with the church's customs are employed by the bride it is helpful, and sometimes necessary, to furnish them with a list of regulations regarding their services for weddings and receptions. Such a list should indicate the precautions to be used in decorating the church, the use of candles, and the prompt removal of decorations and cleaning expected.

Picture Taking and the Reception

The minister in the interview with the bride and groom to discuss the wedding ceremony should offer suggestions for ways they can have pictures made without neglecting their guests who have been invited to the wedding reception. While current practice in many areas calls for immediate picture taking after the ceremony with guests waiting twenty minutes or half an hour for the reception to begin, this is being altered. The joy of the wedding celebration is not dissipated if the bride and groom, when the reception is held at the church, go immediately to the reception hall and cut the cake and begin the reception. Pictures of the cake cutting are made. Then the bridal party returns to the sanctuary for pictures. After this they go back to the reception to receive guests formally in a receiving line or to greet their guests informally. In some churches the bride and groom receive guests in the vestibule as guests leave the sanctuary. The wedding party goes to the reception and then returns to the sanctuary for pictures later. Or pictures may be posed early before guests arrive for the wedding.

It is standard practice to prohibit flash pictures until the bride and groom have proceeded to the rear of the church. Time exposures are permitted if they can be made without disturbing the ceremony or guests. One church's policy stipulates that a photographer is welcome exactly to the extent that he makes himself inconspicuous.

Candid shots of the celebration usually give a collection of pictures which include almost everyone. They can be made by an unobtrusive professional or competent amateur without disrupting the joy of the occasion. The minister should inform the photographer of the church's customs to insure his being fully familiar with them.

Sound Recording the Ceremony

The minister may suggest that the couple consider having a sound recording made of the music and ceremony which can later be put on a phonograph record. Some professional services offer this for a fee. Or a good tape recorder set for 7 inches per second can be used. Some ministers make the tape recording and give it to the couple as a wedding gift along with a written copy of the service.

Wedding Bulletin

The use of a wedding bulletin is becoming more common. A bulletin announces to the wedding guests that this is a worship service and serves as a memento of the occasion. It also indicates the wedding music, members of the wedding party, and what participation, if any, is expected of the guests in the wedding service. Often a brief prayer for the couple is written on the back of the bulletin. Many beautiful and attractive designs for bulletin covers are available. They can be either mimeographed or printed. Samples can be had free of charge from the following companies:

Sacred Design Associates
840 Colorado Ave., South
Minneapolis, Minn. 55416

Conception Abbey Press
Conception, Mo. 64433

The Liturgical Press
Collegeville, Minn. 56321

Local church supply houses can furnish attractive samples also.

Honorarium for the Minister

In most parts of the country it is still customary for the groom to give the minister or ministers performing the ceremony a monetary token of gratitude. Some ministers refuse honoraria for weddings. Others accept honoraria graciously. One minister keeps a record of the amount received and the date of the wedding. He returns the honorarium on the first anniversary of the couple's wedding with a note asking them to use it for an evening out as his guest! Others give the honorarium to their wives or buy a present for the couple with it. If the minister has qualms of conscience about accepting honoraria he might use it for buying several books on marriage and family living to give the couple as they begin a home.

Alcohol

The church's policy should indicate whether or not alcohol may be served at receptions in the church. One Episcopal church does not allow alcohol at receptions in the church in order to give families the option of a church wedding and reception without the expense of furnishing champagne for all the guests. The same church's wedding policy states: "It is not in order for any member of the bridal party to come into the church for the wedding or for the rehearsal after having had anything alcoholic to drink." Local customs vary in regard to the use of alcohol, but the church should make known its policy in this regard to prevent embarrassment or misunderstanding.

Smoking

Smoking is generally not allowed in the sanctuary or chapel at any time. Fire regulations and local custom may prohibit it elsewhere, but this should be indicated. Florists should be advised not to smoke in the sanctuary or chapel where a stray spark on a carpet may cause a fire.

Rice and Confetti

These are usually not permitted in the church because of the difficulty involved in cleaning up after they are thrown.

Sample Policy Statement for Weddings and Receptions*

The Directory of the Worship and Work of the Church (Presbyterian Church, U.S.) states: "Since marriage is a divine institution, established by God in creation, the Church solemnizes marriage in holy worship, with prayer and blessings, bearing witness to its

* This sample is used by permission of Billy J. Christian, Minister of Music, Idlewild Presbyterian Church, Memphis, Tennessee.

nature, and also requires vows concerning their obligation to God from those who engage in it. As they are enjoined to marry in the Lord, Christians should have their marriage solemnized by a lawful Minister of the Word, ordinarily in the building set apart to the worship of God and in the presence of God's people."

The Idlewild Presbyterian Church welcomes the opportunity of sharing with you in making your wedding plans. Our sanctuary, chapel, and other facilities, as well as our staff personnel are at your service. This booklet is offered in the hope that it may aid in your planning.

Minister—Arrange an appointment to discuss the dates you have chosen for the wedding and the wedding rehearsal, to be sure he is free to perform the ceremony and to reserve the sanctuary or chapel and any other necessary facilities. Ordinarily, weddings performed in Idlewild are conducted by one of its ministers. If another minister is to be invited to conduct the ceremony, or to share in the service, the invitation to him should properly be extended by one of the ministers of Idlewild Church.

Counseling—The ministers will want to counsel with you further than simply setting a date. Arrange for these conferences early, before parties and other details crowd the calendar.

Date—Your wedding date can be made final only *after* you have determined that the church calendar and the minister's schedule will allow for the date you have in mind. You will not be able to have invitations printed until this is done. Sundays and Thursdays are heavily scheduled with church activities so that weddings and rehearsals should not be set on these days.

Organist—Arrange to consult with him concerning the music appropriate to the wedding as a service of Christian worship of the church. It is expected that our church organist will play for all weddings where music is desired.

Music for Christian marriage—Music is not necessary at a wedding, but most brides feel that it adds much to the beauty of the ceremony. This music is not primarily an entertainment or a "cover" for the seating of guests; it is to set the mood for worship. Therefore, the music should have no secular associations, but rather be standard organ literature used in services of worship. The organist will recommend appropriate music in your conference.

The Directory for the Worship and Work of the Church says "such music as accompanies the service should be to the glory of God who sanctifies marriage, to which end the use of hymns by the congregation is appropriate."

Solos, hymns—Texts of vocal music should be considered more than a favorite melody. Songs that are clearly secular in their celebration of love (such as "I Love You Truly," "Because," "At Dawning," etc.) are very appropriately sung at a reception, but not at the ceremony.

The Lord's Prayer is said by the minister, bridal party, and congregation all together, as an act of worship in the ceremony. It is the first prayer said together by bride and groom as husband and wife. It is a personal prayer to be prayed by individuals and should not be dramatized by a musical setting.

It is suggested that congregational singing of hymns at the wedding ceremony be considered since the hymns of the church express the thoughts of Christian hearts in worship. Let the congregation join with you in prayers and praises.

If a soloist is desired, arrangements should be made for rehearsing with the organist at some time other than at the wedding rehearsal.

Photographer—No photographs are to be taken in the church before or during the wedding ceremony. If a reception is to be held at the church, it is suggested that taking pictures after the ceremony be limited in order not to keep your guests waiting.

Florist—The florist should be acquainted with the sanctuary or chapel and the requests of this church:

In the sanctuary, floral arrangements in the front center must be so arranged that the organist's mirror view of the center aisle and door is unobstructed. The electrical signals are simply an aid of this visual contact with the procession.

If a kneeling bench is desired, the church has one available, or the florist can supply one.

Flowers and candles should enhance the

beauty of our sanctuary and chapel rather than hide it.

Candles must be of the nondrip variety and have a protective covering on the floors; proper precautions should be taken for safety. Be sure someone is delegated to see that the candles are lighted and that he knows where the lighting taper is located!

If you desire to leave any flowers for church use or for distribution to the sick, arrangements should be made in the church office. All wedding decorations other than flowers left for such purposes must be removed immediately following the service.

It is expected that NO RICE OR CONFETTI will be thrown within the buildings, please.

The rehearsal—This is usually scheduled the night before the wedding is to take place, and at a time prior to any rehearsal dinner. This avoids having to rush the meal to get to a later rehearsal on time. Set the time when all parties involved can be present, and arrive promptly. This rehearsal is a time of careful preparation for a service of worship. The bride who participates in the rehearsal in her proper role is the one who will best know and understand the proceedings of the wedding ceremony.

If a wedding consultant, or florist acting in that capacity is used, it is to be understood that the minister will direct the wedding rehearsal, with the assistance of the consultant.

Attendants—Relatives and friends of your faith would be first choice. Experience has shown that the use of children in a bridal party is not always wise. Consider the ability of the little flower girl or ringbearer to participate worshipfully in your Christian wedding service. If you choose to have either or both, they may be seated with their parents after the procession.

The wedding day—If a wedding is scheduled for "three o'clock," this means that the musical prelude and vocal music will have finished and the bridal processional will begin at three o'clock. One-half hour before this, the groom, best man, and ushers should arrive at the church. The ushers begin their duties while the groom and the best man wait in the room designated by the minister at the rehearsal.

Facilities are available for the ladies to dress

at the church if they wish. Plan to arrive early enough to have plenty of time.

Reception—Facilities of the church are at your disposal if they are desired for a reception. Consult the church hostess as early as possible concerning details of the reception if it is to be held at the church.

Costs—Plan your wedding wisely; modest arrangements which you can afford are more desirable than beginning your married life in debt. A church wedding involves certain basic costs aside from your clothing, invitations, dinners, and the like. The following may answer some questions and serve as a guide:

Pastor—no charge. An honorarium is acceptable.

Organist—no charge. An honorarium is acceptable.

Soloist—the church does not take responsibility for securing or paying the soloist. This is handled by the bride. The organist is in a position to recommend singers if you wish. Financial arrangements should be concluded at the time of making the date with the singer.

Use of Sanctuary, Chapel, Reception Rooms

—There is no charge for the use of the facilities of the church; however, there is the cost of extra help needed in preparing and cleaning afterward. For the specific needs of your wedding and reception, consult the church hostess. The size and time may call for more help, but this list will give some idea of expected costs.

Sample Fees
[Local churches policy committee will set exact amounts]

Cleaning of sanctuary after the ceremony

Reception in lecture hall (service of hostess, janitors, dishwashers, but not including food)

Cleaning of Trippeer Chapel after ceremony

Reception in Parlor (100 persons or less)

Checklist

   1. Meet with minister for date-setting and premarital counseling:
      Date _____ Time _____ Place _____

   2. Date and time approved by the church and placed on church calendar?_____

   3. Appointment with organist:
      Date _____ Time _____ Place _____

4. If soloist is desired, contact (*after* consultation with organist) the singer concerning selections desired and arrange for honorarium figure.

   Singer _____ Phone _____
   Selections:
   1. _____ by _____
   2. _____ by _____
   Costs _____ Address _____

5. Rehearsal for organist and singer:
   Date _____ Time _____ Place _____

6. Photographer _____ Phone _____

7. Florist _____ Phone _____
   Be sure he is familiar with church rules.

8. Is florist to help at the rehearsal?_____
   the wedding?_____

9. Who lights the candles? (florist, usher, janitor)

10. Has that person been so informed and acquainted with use and location of the tapers?_____

11. Consultation with church hostess on reception details:
    Date _____ Time _____ Place _____

12. Secure your license?_____
    Give this to the minister at the rehearsal.

Notes and Reminders

PART II

A CLASSICAL WEDDING SERVICE

The United Methodist Service*
The Order for the Service of Marriage

The minister is enjoined diligently to instruct those requesting his offices for their prospective marriage in the Christian significance of the holy estate into which they seek to enter.

All arrangements pertaining to the service of marriage shall be made in full consultation with the minister.

This service may begin with a prelude, anthem, solo, or hymn. It may include a processional and recessional and be concluded with a postlude.[1]

---

* From *The Book of Worship for Church and Home.* Copyright © 1964, 1965 by Board of Publication of The Methodist Church, Inc. Used by permission.

[1] Suggested music from *The Book of Hymns:*
Processional: "Praise the Lord! ye heavens, adore him"; "For the beauty of the earth"; "Praise to the Lord, the Almighty"; "Praise, my soul, the King of heaven."

117

The congregation shall stand as the wedding procession begins.

The Christian names of the bride and bridegroom may be used in place of "this man and this woman" in the first, third, and fourth paragraphs.

When the Sacrament of the Lord's Supper is requested, this service should be provided at a time other than the service of marriage.

At the time appointed, the persons to be married, having been qualified according to the laws of the state and the standards of the Church, standing together facing the minister, the man at the minister's left hand and the woman at the right hand, the minister shall say,

Dearly beloved, we are gathered together here in the sight of God, and in the presence of these witnesses, to join together *this man and this woman* in holy matrimony; which is an

---

Recessional: "Now thank we all our God"; "Joyful, joyful, we adore thee," "God is love; his mercy brightens"; "Love divine, all loves excelling."

Prayers and hymns: "May the grace of Christ our Savior"; "Blessed Jesus, at thy word"; "The King of love my Shepherd is"; "O perfect Love, all human thought transcending."

honorable estate, instituted of God, and signifying unto us the mystical union which exists between Christ and his Church; which holy estate Christ adorned and beautified with his presence in Cana of Galilee. It is therefore not to be entered into unadvisedly, but reverently, discreetly, and in the fear of God. Into this holy estate these two persons come now to be joined. If any man can show just cause why they may not lawfully be joined together, let him now speak, or else hereafter forever hold his peace.

Addressing the persons to be married, the minister shall say,

I require and charge you both, as you stand in the presence of God, before whom the secrets of all hearts are disclosed, that, having duly considered the holy covenant you are about to make, you do now declare before this company your pledge of faith, each to the other. Be well assured that if these solemn vows are kept inviolate, as God's Word demands, and if steadfastly you endeavor to do the will of your heavenly Father, God will bless your marriage, will grant you fulfillment in it, and will establish your home in peace.

Then shall the minister say to the man, using his Christian name,

N., wilt thou have this woman to be thy wedded wife, to live together in the holy estate of matrimony? Wilt thou love her, comfort her, honor and keep her, in sickness and in health; and forsaking all other keep thee only unto her so long as ye both shall live?

The man shall answer,

I will.

Then shall the minister say to the woman, using her Christian name,

N., wilt thou have this man to be thy wedded husband, to live together in the holy estate of matrimony? Wilt thou love him, comfort him, honor and keep him, in sickness and in health; and forsaking all other keep thee only unto him so long as ye both shall live?

The woman shall answer,

I will.

Then shall the minister say,

Who giveth this woman to be married to this man?

The father of the woman, or whoever gives her in marriage, shall answer,

I do.

Then, the minister, receiving the hand of the woman from her father or other sponsor, shall cause the man with his right hand to take the woman by her right hand, and say after him,

I, N., take thee, N., to be my wedded wife, to have and to hold, from this day forward, for better, for worse, for richer, for poorer, in sickness and in health, to love and to cherish, till death us do part, according to God's holy ordinance; and thereto I pledge thee my faith.

Then shall they loose their hands; and the woman, with her right hand taking the man by his right hand, shall say after the minister,

I, N., take thee, N., to be my wedded husband, to have and to hold, from this day forward, for better, for worse, for richer, for poorer, in sickness and in health, to love and to cherish, till death us do part, according to God's holy ordinance; and thereto I pledge thee my faith.

Then they may give to each other rings, or the man may give to the woman a ring, in this wise: the minister, taking the ring or rings, shall say,

The wedding ring is the outward and visible sign of an inward and spiritual grace, signifying to all the uniting of his man and woman in holy matrimony, through the Church of Jesus Christ our Lord.

Then the minister may say,

Let us pray.
Bless, O Lord, the giving of these rings, that they who wear them may abide in thy peace, and continue in thy favor; through Jesus Christ our Lord. **Amen.**

Or, if there be but one ring, the minister say,

Bless, O Lord, the giving of this ring, that he who gives it and she who wears it may abide forever in thy peace, and continue in thy favor; through Jesus Christ our Lord. **Amen.**

The minister shall then deliver the proper ring to the man to put upon the third finger of the woman's left hand. The man, holding the ring there, shall say after the minister,

In token and pledge of our constant faith and abiding love, with this ring I thee wed,

in the name of the Father, and of the Son, and of the Holy Spirit. Amen.

Then, if there is a second ring, the minister shall deliver it to the woman to put upon the third finger of the man's left hand; and the woman, holding the ring there, shall say after the minister,

In token and pledge of our constant faith and abiding love, with this ring I thee wed, in the name of the Father, and of the Son, and of the Holy Spirit. Amen.

Then shall the minister join their right hands together and, with his hand on their united hands, shall say,

Forasmuch as *N.* and *N.* have consented together in holy wedlock, and have witnessed the same before God and this company, and thereto have pledged their faith each to the other, and have declared the same by joining hands and by giving and receiving *rings;* I pronounce that they are husband and wife together, in the name of the Father, and of the Son, and of the Holy Spirit. Those whom God hath joined together, let not man put asunder. **Amen.**

Then shall the minister say,

Let us pray.

Then shall the husband and wife kneel; the minister shall say,

O eternal God, creator and preserver of all mankind, giver of all spiritual grace, the author of everlasting life: Send thy blessing upon this man and this woman, whom we bless in thy name; that they may surely perform and keep the vow and covenant between them made, and may ever remain in perfect love and peace together, and live according to thy laws.

Look graciously upon them, that they may love, honor, and cherish each other, and so live together in faithfulness and patience, in wisdom and true godliness, that their home may be a haven of blessing and a place of peace; through Jesus Christ our Lord. **Amen.**

Then the husband and wife, still kneeling, shall join with the minister and congregation in the Lord's Prayer, saying,

Our Father, who art in heaven, hallowed be thy name. Thy kingdom come, thy will be done on earth as it is in heaven. Give us this day our daily bread. And forgive us our trespasses, as we forgive those who trespass

against us. And lead us not into temptation, but deliver us from evil. For thine is the kingdom, and the power, and the glory, forever. Amen.

Then the minister shall give this blessing,

God the Father, the Son, and the Holy Spirit bless, preserve, and keep you; the Lord graciously with his favor look upon you, and so fill you with all spiritual benediction and love that you may so live together in this life that in the world to come you may have life everlasting. **Amen.**

CONTEMPORARY WEDDING SERVICES

A Baptist Service*

Organ Recital
"Like A Shepherd God Doth
Guide Us" .... Bach
"Now Thank We All Our God" .. Kaufman
Air from Suite for Strings
No. 3 in D Major ...... Bach-Phillips
"Praise to the Lord,
the Almighty" .... Drischner
"Jesu Joy of Man's Desiring" . Bach-Grace
The Doxology .... Genevan Psalter

Processional
"A Mighty Fortress is Our God"
Luther-Pachelbel

The Call to Worship
"How beautiful upon the mountains are the
feet of him that brings good tidings, that pub-

* This service used by permission of the Rev. and Mrs. Deryl Ray Fleming and Dr. Wayne E. Oates, Professor of Psychology of Religion, Southern Baptist Theological Seminary, Louisville, Ky.

lishes peace." The people everywhere and in all ages have been drawn together in times of tribulation and likewise in times of joy. Thus have we from far places been drawn together this day to witness and to commemorate with a man and a woman their union for the founding among us of a new home. There is in this sacred hour a reverence which moves us to a spirit of worship.

(Let us stand and sing together)

The Hymn   Praise to the Lord, the Almighty

(Let us pray)

The Invocation

O Lord, open thou our lips, and our mouth shall show forth thy praise; open thou our minds that we may be enlightened by the truth of thy gospel; open thou our hearts that we may receive the fullness of thy grace; through Jesus Christ our Lord. Amen.

(Let us read responsively)

The Reading . . . . Psalm 67

May God be gracious to us and bless us and
    make his face to shine upon us,

That thy ways may be known upon earth,
thy saving power among all nations.

Let the people praise thee, O God; let all
the people praise thee!

Let the nations be glad and sing for joy,
for thou dost judge the peoples with
equity and guide the nations upon earth.

Let the peoples praise thee, O God, let all
the peoples praise thee!

The earth has yielded its increase; God, our
God, has blessed us.

God has blessed us; let all the ends of the
earth fear him!

Glory be to the Father, and to the Son, and
to the Holy Ghost; as it was in the beginning, is now, and ever shall be, world
without end. Amen.

(Let us pray together the prayer our Lord
taught us to pray, saying . . .)

The Lord's Prayer

Our Father which art in heaven, Hallowed
be thy name. Thy kingdom come. Thy will
be done in earth as it is in heaven. Give us this
day our daily bread. And forgive us our trespasses as we forgive those who trespass against
us. And lead us not into temptation, but deliver

us from evil: For thine is the kingdom, and the power, and the glory, for ever. Amen.

(Hear the reading of the Word of God as it is found in the Moffatt Translation of I Cor. 13:4-8; 13.)

The Reading of the Scripture

Love is very patient, very kind. Love knows no jealousy; love makes no parade, gives itself no airs, is never rude, never selfish, never irritated, never resentful; love is never glad when others go wrong, love is gladdened by goodness, always slow to expose, always eager to believe the best, always hopeful, always patient. Love never disappears. Thus faith and hope and love last on, these three, but the greatest of these is love.

Choral Worship   Organist and Choir
   "O Lord, Most Holy" . . . . Franck

The Service of Holy Matrimony

Dearly beloved, we are gathered together here in the presence of God and in the fellowship of this Christian community to join together this man and this woman in Christian marriage. Christian marriage is a covenant of faith and trust between a man and a woman, established within their shared commitment in the covenant of faith in Jesus Christ as Lord. Therefore, it requires of both man and woman openness of life and thought, freedom from doubt and suspicion, and commitment to speak the truth in love as they grow up into Christ who is the head of the Church. Christian marriage, furthermore, is a covenant of hope that endures all things in which both husband and wife commit themselves to interpret each other's behavior with understanding and compassion, and never give up trying to communicate with each other. Christian marriage, therefore, is a covenant of love in which both husband and wife empty themselves of their own concerns and take upon themselves the concerns of each other in loving each other as Christ loved the Church and gave himself for it. Therefore, this covenant is not to be entered into unadvisedly or lightly, but reverently, discreetly, advisedly, and soberly in the fear of God. Into this holy estate these two persons come now to be joined.

(*Groom*), will you have (*Bride*) to be your wedded wife, to live together in the covenant of faith, hope, and love according to the intention of God for your lives together in Jesus Christ? Will you listen to her inmost thoughts, be considerate and tender in your care of her, and stand by her faithfully in sickness and in health, and, preferring her above all others, accept full responsibility for her every necessity as long as you both shall live?

(*Bride*), will you have (*Groom*) to be your wedded husband, to live together in the covenant of faith, hope, and love according to the intention of God for your lives together in Jesus Christ? Will you listen to his inmost thoughts, be considerate and helpful in your support of him, and stand by him faithfully in sickness and in health, and, preferring him above all others, accept full responsibility for his every necessity as long as you both shall live?

Who gives (*Bride*) to be married to (*Groom*)?

(Party moves to platform)

(*Groom*) and (*Bride*), will you now express your vows to each other?

The Vows

I, (*Bride/Groom*), take you, (*Groom/*

Bride), to be my wedded husband/wife, to have and to hold from this day forward, for better, for worse, for richer for poorer, in sickness and in health, to love and to understand, till death shall part us, according to the design of God in creation and commit myself completely to you.

The Ring Ceremony

With this ring I thee wed in the name of the Father and the Son and the Holy Spirit.

(Let us pray)

The Prayer of Dedication

Eternal God, make us instruments of thy peace; where hate rules, let us bring love; where malice, forgiveness; where disputes, reconciliation; where error, truth; where doubt, belief; where sorrow, joy. O Lord, let us strive more to comfort others than to be comforted; to understand others more than to be understood; to love others more than to be loved! For he who gives, receives; he who forgets himself, finds; he who forgives, receives forgiveness; and dying we arise again to eternal life through Jesus Christ our Lord. Amen.

The Pronunciation

For as much as (*Groom*) and (*Bride*) have consented together in holy wedlock, and have witnessed the same before God and in the fellowship of this Christian community, and have committed themselves completely to each other, and have declared this by the giving and receiving of the rings, I pronounce that they are husband and wife in the name of the Father and the Son and the Holy Spirit. Amen.

(Let us pray)

Choral Benediction   Choir
    "The Lord Bless Thee and
       Keep Thee" . . . . Lutkin

Recessional
    Toccata, Symphony V . . . . Widor

Episcopal Service*
for Trial Use

Concerning the Service

Christian Marriage is a solemn and public covenant between a man and a woman. In the

* From *Services for Trial Use,* copyright 1971 by Charles Mortimer Guilbert as Custodian of the Standard Book of Common Prayer. By permission.

Episcopal Church it is required that one, at least, of the parties must be a baptized Christian; that the ceremony be attested by at least two witnesses; and that the marriage conform to the laws of the State and the Canons of this Church.

A priest or a bishop normally presides at the Celebration and Blessing of a Marriage, because such Ministers alone have the function of pronouncing the nuptial Blessing, and of celebrating the Holy Eucharist.

When both a bishop and a priest are present and officiating, the bishop should pronounce the Blessing and preside at the Eucharist.

A deacon, or an assisting priest, may deliver the charge and ask for the declaration of intention, read the Gospel, and perform other assisting functions at the Eucharist.

Where it is permitted by civil law that deacons may perform marriages, and no priest or bishop is available, the deacon may use the service which follows, omitting only the priestly Blessing, beginning, "God the Father, God the Son . . ."

It is desirable that Lessons from the Old Testament and the Epistles be read by lay persons and that the newly married couple present the offerings of Bread and wine at the Offertory.

In the opening exhortation (at the symbol of *N.N.*), the full names of the persons to be married are to be declared. Subsequently, only their Christian names are used.

The Celebration and Blessing of a Marriage

At the time appointed, the persons to be married, with their witnesses, assemble with the Minister in the church or some other appropriate place.

During their entrance, a Psalm, Hymn, or Anthem may be sung; or instrumental music may be used.

Then the presiding Minister, facing the People and the persons to be married, with the woman on his right and the man on his left, addresses the congregation and says

Good people, we have come together in the presence of God to witness and proclaim the joining together of this man and this woman in marriage. The bond of marriage was established by God at creation, and our Lord Jesus

Christ himself adorned this manner of life by his presence and first miracle at a wedding in Cana of Galilee. It signifies to us the union between Christ and his Church, and Holy Scripture commends it to be honored among all men.

The union of man and woman in heart, body, and mind is intended by God for their mutual joy; for the help and comfort given one another in prosperity and adversity; and, when it is God's will, for the procreation of children and their nurture in the knowledge and love of the Lord. Therefore marriage is not to be entered into unadvisedly or lightly, but reverently, deliberately, and in accord with the purposes for which it was instituted by God.

Into this holy union *N.N.* and *N.N.* come now to be joined. If any of you can show just cause why they may not lawfully be married, speak now, or for ever hold your peace.

Then the Minister says to the persons to be married

I require and charge you both in the Name of God, that if either of you know any reason why you may not be united in marriage lawfully and in accordance with God's Word, you confess it now.

The Minister then says to the man

N., Will you have this woman to be your wife, to live together in a holy marriage? Will you love her, comfort her, honor and keep her, in sickness and in health, and forsaking all others, be faithful to her as long as you both shall live?

The man answers

I will by God's help.

The Minister then says to the woman

N., Will you have this man to be your husband to live together in a holy marriage? Will you love him, comfort him, honor and keep him in sickness and in health, and forsaking all others, be faithful to him as long as you both shall live?

The woman answers

I will by God's help.

The Minister addresses the following question to the wedding party and congregation:

Will you who witness these vows do all in

your power to support and uphold this marriage in the years ahead?

Answer
We will.

Here the Minister may ask

Who gives this woman to be married to this
man?

The father, or a friend, says

I do.

*The Minister receives the woman at her
father's or friend's hand and causes the man
to take the woman's right hand in his.*

*The presiding Minister then says to the Peo-
ple*

Minister   The Lord be with you.
Answer   And also with you.
Minister   Let us pray.

THE COLLECT   *the People standing*
Eternal God, creator and sustainer of all men,

giver of all grace, author of salvation: Look with favor upon this man and this woman, that they may grow in love and peace together; through Jesus Christ your Son our Lord, who lives and reigns with you in the unity of the Holy Spirit, one God, now and for ever. *Amen.*

Then one or more of the following passages from Holy Scripture is read. If there is to be a Communion, a passage from the Gospels is always included.

THE LESSON	THE GOSPEL
Genesis 2:4-9, 15-24	Mark 10:6-9
Colossians 3:12-17	Matthew 7:21, 24-29
Ephesians 5:20-33	
1 Corinthians 13	Matthew 5:13-16
1 John 4:7-16	John 15:11-17

Between the Readings, Psalm 128, 113, or 100, or some other Psalm, Hymn, or Anthem may be sung or said.

After the Readings (or after the homily if there is one), the Service continues with

THE MARRIAGE

All stand, and the man facing the woman, and taking her right hand in his, says

I, *N.*, take you, *N.*, to be my wife, to have and to hold from this day forward, for better for worse, for richer for poorer, in sickness and in health, to love and to cherish, until we are parted by death. This is my solemn vow.

Then they loose their hands and the woman, still facing the man, takes his right hand in hers and says

I, *N.*, take you, *N.*, to be my husband, to have and to hold from this day forward, for better for worse, for richer for poorer, in sickness and in health, to love and to cherish, until we are parted by death. This is my solemn vow.

They loose their hands.

The Minister may ask God's blessing on the ring (or rings) as follows:

Bless, O Lord, this ring that *he* who gives it and *she* who wears it may live in your peace, and continue in your favor, all the days of their life; through Jesus Christ our Lord. *Amen.*

The giver places the ring on the ring-finger of the other's hand, and says,

N., I give you this ring as a symbol of my vow, and with all that I am, and all that I have, I honor you, in the Name of God.

Then the Minister joins the right hands of the husband and wife and says

Now that *N.* and *N.* have given themselves to each other by solemn vows, with the joining of hands and the giving and receiving of *a ring* (rings), I pronounce that they are husband and wife, in the Name of the Father, and of the Son, and of the Holy Spirit.
Those whom God has joined together let not man put asunder.

The Congregation responds Amen.

Communion is to be celebrated here.

When there is no Communion, the Service continues on the following page.

THE BLESSING OF THE MARRIAGE
The Minister says

Let us pray together in the words our Savior taught us:

Standing, all say

Our Father in heaven,
  holy be your Name,
  your kingdom come,
  your will be done,
    on earth as in heaven.
Give us today our daily bread.
Forgive us our sins
  as we forgive those who sin against us.
Do not bring us to the test
  but deliver us from evil.
For the kingdom, the power, and the glory are
  yours now and for ever. Amen.

The Minister says this prayer over the couple:

Almighty God, look graciously, we pray, on this man and this woman, and on all whom you make to be one flesh in holy marriage. Make their lives together a sacrament of your love to this broken world, so that unity may overcome estrangement, forgiveness heal guilt, and joy triumph over despair; in the Name of our Lord Jesus Christ, to whom be all honor and glory, now and forever. *Amen.*

He may then add one or more of the following three prayers:

Almighty God, Creator of mankind, the source of all life, grant to *N.* and *N.*, if it be your will, the gift and heritage of children, and the grace to nurture them in the knowledge and love of your Name; through Jesus Christ our Lord. *Amen.*

Almighty God, giver of life and love, bless *N.* and *N.* whom you have now joined in holy matrimony. Grant them wisdom and devotion in the ordering of their common life that each may be to the other a strength in need, a counsellor in perplexity, a comfort in sorrow, and a companion in joy. And so knit their wills together in your will, and their spirits in your spirit, that they may live together in love and in peace all the days of their life, through Jesus Christ our Lord. *Amen*

Almighty God, by whose love the whole world is created, sustained and redeemed, so fill *N.* and *N.* with the overflowing abundance of your grace that their lives may reflect your compassion for all men. May their love for each other not blind them to the brokenness in the world.

As you teach them to bind up each other's wounds, teach them also to heal the hurts of others. As their mutual respect orders their common life within the family, direct them to their share also in the shaping of a society in which human dignity may flourish and abound. At all times and in all seasons may they rejoice to serve you and to give you thanks, through Jesus Christ our Lord. *Amen.*

The following prayer is always added, the couple kneeling:

O God, who consecrated the state of Marriage to be a sign of the spiritual unity between Christ and his Church; Bless these your servants, that they may love, honor, and cherish each other in faithfulness and patience, in wisdom and true godliness, and that their home may be a haven of blessing and of peace; through Jesus Christ our Lord, who lives and reigns with you and the Holy Spirit, one God, now and for ever. *Amen.*

The husband and wife still kneeling, the Priest pronounces this nuptial Blessing:

God the Father, God the Son, God the Holy

Spirit, bless, preserve and keep you; the Lord mercifully with his favor look upon you and fill you with all spiritual benediction and grace, that you may faithfully live together in this life, and in the world to come have life everlasting. *Amen.*

The Peace may now be exchanged.

As the wedding party leaves the Church, a Psalm, Hymn, or Anthem may be sung; or instrumental music may be used.

One of the Ministers may dismiss the Congregation.

AT THE EUCHARIST:
THE BLESSING OF THE MARRIAGE
For the Intercession, the Deacon or person appointed says

Almighty God, in whom we live and move and have our being: Look graciously upon the world which you have made, and on the Church for which your Son gave his life; and especially on all whom you make to be one flesh in holy marriage:

Grant that their lives together may be a sacrament of your love to this broken world, so that unity may overcome estrangement, forgiveness heal guilt, and joy overcome despair. *Amen.*

Grant that *N.* and *N.* may so live together, that the strength of their love may enrich our common life and become an example of your faithfulness. *Amen.*

The following suffrages may be omitted:

Grant that they may have children, if it be your will, and may bring them up by your help to know and love you. *Amen.*

Grant them such fulfillment of their mutual affection that they may reach out in concern for others, to the praise of your Name. *Amen.*

Grant that all married persons who have witnessed this exchange of vows may find their union strengthened and their loyalty confirmed. *Amen.*

Grant that the bonds of our common humanity which unite every man to his neighbor, and the living to the dead, may be transformed by your grace, that justice and peace may prevail and your will be done on earth as it is in heaven. *Amen.*

Then, while the congregation remains standing, the husband and wife kneel, and the Priest says the following prayer:

O God, who consecreated the state of Marriage to be a sign of the spiritual unity between Christ and his Church; Bless these your servants, that they may love, honor, and cherish each other in faithfulness and patience, in wisdom and true godliness, and that their home may be a haven of blessing and of peace; through Jesus Christ our Lord, who lives and reigns with you and the Holy Spirit, one God, now and for ever. *Amen.*

The husband and wife still kneeling, the Priest pronounces this nuptial Blessing:

God the Father, God the Son, God the Holy Spirit, bless, preserve and keep you; the Lord mercifully with his favor look upon you and fill you with all spiritual benediction and grace, that you may faithfully live together in this life, and in the world to come have life everlasting. *Amen.*

The Peace is now exchanged.

The Liturgy continues with the Offertory.

The following Proper Preface may be used at the Eucharist:

TRADITIONAL

Because thou hast ordained the solemn covenant of love between husband and wife as a witness of the union of thy son Jesus Christ with the holy fellowship of all faithful people:

CONTEMPORARY

Because you have ordained the solemn covenant of love between husband and wife as a witness of the union of your son Jesus Christ with the holy fellowship of all faithful people:

Additional Directions and Suggestions

The Celebration and Blessing of a Marriage may be used with any authorized liturgy for the Holy Eucharist. This Order of Service will then replace the Ministry of the Word, and the Eucharist will begin with the Offertory. When this Service is used with the Order for the Holy Communion in the Book of Common Prayer, the Prayer for the Church and the Confession of Sin may be omitted.

After the declaration of intention (betrothal), it is fitting that the man and woman to be married remain where they may conveniently hear the reading of Scripture. They may then approach the altar either for the marriage vows or for the prayers and nuptial Blessing.

It is appropriate that all remain standing until the conclusion of the Collect. Seating may be provided for the wedding party, so that all may be seated for the Lessons and the Homily.

The Apostles' Creed may be recited after the Lessons (or after the Homily, if there is one).

At the Offertory, it is desirable that the bread and wine be offered to the Ministers by the newly married persons. They may then remain before the Lord's Table and receive Holy Communion before other members of the congregation.

At the Peace, the newly married couple shall first greet each other, after which greetings may be exchanged throughout the congregation.

A Lutheran Service*

THE MARRIAGE SERVICE

FIRST FORM

Stand

ENTRANCE HYMN [1]

Presiding
Minister
The grace of our Lord Jesus Christ, the love of God, and the fellowship of the Holy Spirit be with you all.[2]

People   And also with you.

Assisting
Minister
Let us pray.

Eternal God, Father of mankind, as you gladdened the wedding at Cana in Galilee by the presence of your Son, so by his presence now make the occasion of this

* Reproduced from "The Marriage Service: Contemporary Worship 3," © 1972, by permission of the publishers for Inter-Lutheran Commission on Worship, representing the cooperating churches, by copyright owners. Numbers refer to notes starting on p. 178.

wedding one of rejoicing. In your favor look upon *N.* and *N.,* about to be joined in marriage, and grant that they, rejoicing in all your gifts, may at length celebrate with Christ the Bridegroom the marriage feast which has no end.

People   Amen.

All   (Hymn of Praise.[3] For complete text of the hymns, including music. *See* "The Marriage Service: Contemporary Worship 3.)

THE LITURGY OF THE WORD OF GOD

Assisting   FIRST LESSON[4]
Minister

        PSALM[5]

Assisting   SECOND LESSON[6]
Minister

    Stand

All   ALLELUIA[7]

The announcement of the Gospel.

People   We praise you, Christ, our Lord and God.

Presiding Minister   HOLY GOSPEL[8]

People   We praise you, Christ, our Lord and God.

Sit

SERMON[9]

Stand

HYMN OF THE DAY[10]

Sit

THE MARRIAGE

The bride, groom, and the wedding party move from their

*places to stand in front of the
ministers. The parents may
stand behind the couple.*

*Assisting
Minister*   The Lord God in his goodness
created mankind male and fe-
male and by the gift of marriage
founded human community in a
joy that begins now and is
brought to perfection in the life
to come.

*(Assisting
Minister)*   But because of our sin and man's
age-old rebellion, the gladness of
marriage can be overcast and the
gift of the family can become a
burden.

Nevertheless, because in his love
God our Father from the beginning established marriage and
continues still to bless it with his
abundant and ever-present support, we can be sustained in our
weariness and have our joy restored.

Presiding   N. and N., if it is your intention
Minister   to share with each other your
laughter and your tears and all
that the years will bring, by your
promises bind youselves now to
each other as husband and wife.

*The couple face one another
and join hands.*

Groom/   I take you N.,
Bride   to be my wife (husband) from
this day forward,
to join with you and share all that
is to come,
and, with the help of God,
I promise to be faithful to you
as he gives us life together."

*The couple exchange rings with
these words:*

Groom/   This ring is a sign of my love and
Bride   faithfulness.

Stand

The presidng minister places his hand over the joined hands of the bride and groom.

Presiding Minister	N. and N., by their promises before God and in the presence of this congregation, have made themselves husband and wife. Blessed be the Father and the Son and the Holy Spirit now and for ever.[12]

Assisting Minister	N. and N. have been joined by the love of God the Father in the life of the Spirit of Christ, and man must not divide them.

All	Blessed be the Father and the Son and the Holy Spirit now and for ever.

The couple kneel.

Presiding Minister	The Lord God, who created our first parents and established them in marriage, establish and sustain you, that you may find delight in

each other and grow in holy love until your life's end.

People   Amen.

The wedding party may join the parents in saying:[13]

Parents   May you dwell in God's presence for ever, may true and constant love preserve you.[14]

The bride and groom embrace and then exchange the sign of peace with the minister, their parents, and the wedding party. The congregation may also join in exchanging the sign of peace.[15]

After exchanging the sign of peace, the couple and the wedding party return to the places they occupied at the beginning of the service.

Assisting Minister   Let us bless God for all the gifts in which we rejoice today.[16]

Presiding Minister   Lord God of our fathers, constant in mercy, great in faithfulness: with high praise this day we recall your acts of unfailing love, all that in your tenderness you have done for the family of man, your great goodness to the house of Israel, your many acts of love to your people the church.

(Presiding Minister)   We bless you for the joy which your servants, *N.* and *N.,* have found in each other, and for the hope and trust with which they have been established in a new relationship.

Give to us such a sense of your constant love that we may employ all our strength in a life of praise of you whose work alone holds true and endures for ever.

People   Amen.

Assisting Minister   Let us pray for *N.* and *N.* in their life together.

Presiding Minister   Faithful Lord, Father of love, pour down your grace upon *N.* and *N.* that they may fulfill the vows they have made this day and reflect your steadfast love in their life-long faithfulness to each other. From your great store of strength give them power and patience, affection and understanding, courage and love toward you, toward each other, and toward the world that they may continue together in mutual growth according to your will in Jesus Christ our Lord.

People   Amen.

Other intercessions may be offered.

Assisting Minister   Let us pray for all families throughout the world.

Presiding Minister   Gracious Father, you provide in family life a means to renew people for their living of each day.

Make your purposes for marriage known to all the families of the world and especially to us who celebrate at this wedding. Enrich husbands and wives, parents and children, more and more with your grace that, strengthening and supporting each other, they may serve those in need and so move the world closer to the fulfillment of your perfect kingdom, where with your Son Jesus Christ and the Holy Spirit, you live and reign, one God through all ages of ages.

People   Amen.

Sit

THE LITURGY OF THE EUCHARISTIC MEAL

Stand

The bread and wine are brought to the altar and are made ready for the meal.[17]

Presiding The Lord be with you.[18]
Minister

People   And also with you.

Presiding Lift up your hearts.
Minister

People   We lift them up to the Lord.

Presiding Let us give thanks to the Lord
Minister   our God.

People   It is right to give him thanks
            and praise.

Presiding It is our duty and delight at all
Minister   times and in all places to give
            thanks to you O Lord, holy
            Father, almighty and ever-living
            God. For your love is firm as the
            ancient earth, your faithfulness
            fixed as the heavens. Creating and
            enriching and continuing life, you
            created us male and female to ful-
            fill one another; you gave us the
            gift of marriage which embodies

your love and which, even where
your name is not known, pro-
claims the love which you have
for the family of man. And so
with the church on earth and the
hosts of heaven we praise your
Name and join their unending
hymn:

All   (Hymn. For complete text of
the hymns, including music, *see*
"The Marriage Service: Contemporary Worship 3.")

Presiding   THE GREAT THANKSGIVING[19]
Minister

All   Our Father in heaven,
            holy be your Name,
            your kingdom come,
            your will be done,
                on earth as in heaven.
        Give us today our daily bread.
        Forgive us our sins
            as we forgive those who sin
            against us.

Do not bring us to the test
but deliver us from evil.
For the kingdom, the power,
and the glory are yours
now and forever. Amen.*

Sit

*The presiding minister breaks
the bread. The minister and his
assistants receive the bread and
wine and then give them to
those who come to the table.*[20]

*Hymns and other music may
be used during the distribution.*

After all have received:

Stand

Presiding   The Lord Jesus Christ strengthen
Minister   and keep you in his grace.

People   Amen.

* English translation of the Lord's Prayer by The
International Consultation on English Texts.

During the following hymn the table is cleared.

HYMN[21]

Assisting Minister	Lord Jesus Christ, as you freely give yourself to your bride the church, grant that the mystery of the union of man and woman in marriage may reveal to the world the self-giving love which you have for your church.
People	Amen.

The minister blesses the people:

Presiding Minister	Almighty God, Father, (✠) Son and Holy Spirit, direct and keep you in his light and truth and love all the days of your life.
People	Amen.
Assisting Minister	Go in peace. Serve the Lord.[22]

THE MARRIAGE SERVICE
A SECOND FORM

Stand

> *The bride, groom, and the wedding party stand in front of the minister. The parents may stand behind the couple.*

Presiding Minister

The grace of our Lord Jesus Christ, the love of God, and the communion of the Holy Spirit be with you all.[2]

People

And also with you.

Assisting Minister

Let us pray.

Eternal God, Father of mankind, as you gladdened the wedding at Cana in Galilee by the presence of your Son, so by his presence now make the occasion of this wedding one of rejoicing. In your favor look upon *N.* and *N.*, about to be joined in marriage, and grant that they, rejoicing in all your gifts, may at length celebrate with Christ the Bridegroom the marriage feast which has no end.

People   Amen.

Sit

One or more lessons from the Bible may be read.[23]

Assisting Minister   The Lord God in his goodness created mankind male and female and by the gift of marriage founded human community in a joy that begins now and is brought to perfection in the life to come.

(Assisting Minister)   But because of our sin and man's age-old rebellion, the gladness of marriage can be overcast and the gift of the family can become a burden.

Nevertheless, because in his love God our Father from the beginning established marriage and continues still to bless it with his abundant and ever-present support, we can be sustained in our weariness and have our joy restored.

Presiding
Minister

N. and N., if it is your intention to share with each other your laughter and your tears and all that the years will bring, by your promises bind yourselves now to each other as husband and wife.

The couple face one another and join hands.

Groom/
Bride

I take you N., to be my wife (husband) from this day forward, to join with you and share all that is to come, and, with the help of God, I promise to be faithful to you as he gives us life together.[11]

The couple exchange rings with these words:

Groom/ This ring is a sign of my love and
Bride   faithfulness.

Stand

> *The presiding minister places*
> *his hand over the joined hands*
> *of the bride and groom.*

Presiding N. and N., by their promises be-
Minister   fore God and in the presence of
             this congregation, have made
             themselves husband and wife.
             Blessed be the Father and the Son
             and the Holy Spirit now and for
             ever.[12]

Assisting N. and N. have been joined by
Minister   the love of God the Father in the
             life of the Spirit of Christ, and
             man must not divide them.

All   Blessed be the Father and the
             Son and the Holy Spirit now
             and for ever.

> *The couple kneel.*

Presiding   The Lord God, who created our
Minister   first parents and established them
in marriage, establish and sustain
you, that you may find delight in
each other and grow in holy love
until your life's end.

People   Amen.

*The wedding party may join
the parents in saying:* [13]

Parents   May you dwell in God's presence
for ever, may true and constant
love preserve you.[14]

The couple stand.

Assisting   Let us bless God for all the gifts
Minister   in which we rejoice today.[16]

Presiding   Lord God of our fathers, constant
Minister   in mercy, great in faithfulness:
with high praise this day we recall
your acts of unfailing love, all
that in your tenderness you have
done for the family of man, your
great goodness to the house of

Israel, your many acts of love to your people the church.

We bless you for the joy which your servants, N. and N., have found in each other, and for the hope and trust with which they have been established in a new relationship.

(Presiding Minister)   Give to us such a sense of your constant love that we may employ all our strength in a life of praise of you whose work alone holds true and endures for ever.

People   Amen.

Assisting Minister   Let us pray for N. and N. in their life together.

Presiding Minister   Faithful Lord, Father of love, pour down your grace upon N. and N. that they may fulfill the vows they have made this day and reflect your steadfast love in their life-long faithfulness to each other. From your great store of strength give them power and patience, affection and understanding, courage and love toward you, toward each other, and toward the world that they may continue together in mutual growth according to your will in Jesus Christ our Lord.

People   Amen.

Other intercessions may be offered.

Assisting   Let us pray for all families
Minister   throughout the world.

Presiding   Gracious Father, you provide in
Minister   family life a means to renew people for their living of each day. Make your purposes for marriage known to all the families of the world and especially to us who celebrate at this wedding. Enrich husbands and wives, parents and children more and more with your grace that, strengthening

and supporting each other, they
may serve those in need and so
move the world closer to the fulfillment of your perfect kingdom,
where with your Son Jesus Christ
and the Holy Spirit, you live and
reign, one God through all ages
of ages.

People   Amen.

All   Our Father in heaven,
                 holy be your Name,
                 your kingdon come,
                 your will be done,
                     on earth as in heaven.
             Give us today our daily bread.
             Forgive us our sins
                 as we forgive those who sin
                     against us.
             Do not bring us to the test
                 but deliver us from evil.
             For the kingdom, the power,
                 and the glory are yours now
                 and forever. Amen.*

* English translation of the Lord's Prayer by the
International Consultation on English Texts.

Assisting   May almighty God bless you.
Minister

People   Amen.

Assisting   May he direct you all the days of
Minister   your life.

People   Amen.

Presiding   Almighty God, Father, (✠) Son
Minister   and Holy Spirit, direct and keep
                you in his light and truth and love
                all the days of your life.

People   Amen.

ALTERNATE WEDDING PROMISES

N., I take you to be my wife (husband) from
this time onward, to join with you and to share
all that is to come, to give and to receive, to
speak and to listen, to inspire and to respond,
and in all circumstances of our life together
to be loyal to you with my whole life and with
all my being.
I take you, *N.*, to be my wife (husband),
I promise before God and these witnesses to

be your faithful husband (wife), to share with
you in plenty and in want, in joy and in sorrow, in sickness and in health, to forgive and
strengthen you and to join with you so that
together we may serve God and others as long
as we both shall live.

I take you, *N.,* to be my wife (husband),
and these things I promise you: I will be faithful to you and honest with you; I will respect,
trust, help, and care for you; I will share my
life with you; I will forgive you as we have
been forgiven; and I will try with you better to
understand ourselves, the world, and God;
through the best and the worst of what is to
come as long as we live.

[For alternate setting "Hymn of Praise," *see*
"The Marriage Service: Contemporary Worship 3."]

FOR THE LEADERS OF WORSHIP

The Marriage Service is designed to provide
a variety of options. By choosing among these
options, the pastor and the couple may create
an appropriate service of worship and praise of
God fitting to the occasion.

The first form of the service is essentially the rite of Holy Communion (Contemporary Worship: *The Holy Communion*) with "The Marriage" between "The Liturgy of the Word of God" and "The Liturgy of the Eucharistic Meal." God's blessing upon the beginning of a new household is appropriately asked in the assembled family of God, all of whom celebrate the marriage and share the eucharistic banquet—the meal of the family of God. The pastor and the couple are encouraged to use the option possibilities creatively, shaping a service appropriate to their situation.

The second form of the service is an example of a briefer rite. It, too, should be creatively shaped to be appropriate to the specific situation.

The music should be selected for its suitability to a service of praise and thanksgiving. A variety of songs and the use of various instruments is encouraged.

The alternate forms of the promises provide additional options.

ARRANGING FOR THE SERVICE

Those who plan to be married are expected to consult with their pastor not only about the nature of marriage but also about the form of the marriage service. The date and time of the marriage should not be announced before consulting with the pastor.

It is good to publish announcements of weddings in bulletins or parish papers. An appropriate form is:

> *N. N.* and *N. N.* have announced their intention to marry on _____, and ask for your prayers.

It is suggested that marriage celebrations are inappropriate during Holy Week because of the solemn character of that time.

Renewal of wedding promises, as a reminder of the covenant to which married people have bound themselves, is appropriate during regular services, especially on those Sundays when the appointed gospel deals with such stories as the holy family or the wedding at Cana.

LEADERSHIP

The Marriage Service is led by a *Presiding Minister* and an *Assisting Minister* (or assisting ministers). The assisting ministers may be lay people. Members of the families of the bride and groom and the wedding party are encouraged to take part in the service: reading lessons, leading prayers, bringing gifts of bread and wine to the altar, administering the chalice. If there are no assisting ministers, the presiding minister assumes their functions.

MUSIC

The Marriage Service is an order of worship of the church. The music, therefore, should be carefully and discriminatingly chosen.

Music within the Marriage Service is discussed in "Notes on the Services": see notes 1, 3, 5, 7, 10, 21, and 22.

There are a number of musical options possible before the entrance procession: music with text sung by a single voice, duet, small ensemble, or full choir; organ music; other instrumental music; and music using a combination of these media. The bibliographies below provide some specific suggestions.[1]

---

[1] *Music for Church Weddings,* Belwin-Mills Publishing Corp.

Planning the Christian Wedding, Paul M. Krause, Concordia Publishing House

Recommended Music for the Marriage Service, Augsburg Publishing House

Wedding Music, Regina H. Fryxell, Fortress Press

Texts of vocal or choral selections should be in harmony with the themes and moods of the Marriage Service itself; for example, the praise of God, God's steadfast love in Christ for his church as the foundation and model for love and fidelity in marriage, the asking of God's presence and blessing. (See the texts of the rite itself, and the texts of the suggested biblical readings and hymns.)

Organ music may be based on hymn-tunes used within the Marriage Service. A printed wedding folder helps to establish such themes and relationships for the congregation. Instrumental music may be selected from chamber music literature or similar sources and should reflect the mood of joy and celebration in the service. Voice(s) and instruments could be joined in solo or choral cantatas.

When organ processional music is desired, it might be in the form of a hymn- or chorale-prelude based upon a hymn to be sung immediately after. This plan also serves the function of introducing the hymn-tune to the congregation.

Wherever employed in the service, and by whatever instruments or voices, the music chosen should: a) be high-quality examples of the art of composition; b) not cloud communication of the content and mood of the service with musical triteness or associations bordering on sentimentality; and c) be within the ability of the performers at hand to play or sing with assurance.

NOTES ON THE SERVICES

The numbers correspond to the numbered parts of the rites themselves.

1. The entrance procession may be preceded by those bearing a cross, candles, banners. The ministers (and the groom) may enter in the procession or directly from the sacristy. When the ministers enter in the procession they precede the wedding party and the bride and groom may enter at the end of the procession, the position of honor. Members of the wedding party might occupy the front pews or be given special chairs in an appropriate location near the chancel.

Suggested entrance hymns:

"The King of love my shepherd is"
(*Service Book and Hymnal* 530,
The Lutheran Hymnal 431)

"Lord, who at Cana's wedding feast"
(*SBH* 301, *TLH* 620)

"Only-begotten, Word of God eternal"
(*Worship Supplement* 772)

"Praise, my soul, the King of heaven"
(*SBH* 160)

"Praise to the Lord, the Almighty"
(*SBH* 408, *TLH* 39)

While singing hymns is encouraged, the
procession may be to instrumental music.

The wedding party is part of the congregation and should stand and sit at the appropriate times.

2. The members of the wedding party having
   arrived at their appointed places, the
   presiding minister greets the people and
   they respond.

   The prayer gathers New Testament refer-
   ences to the joy of marriage in the context
   of the relationship of Christ the Bridegroom to the church, his bride.

3. The HYMN OF PRAISE is from Psalm 89:1, Jeremiah 33:11, and Psalm 100:5. It joyfully relates the promises of fidelity in marriage to the steadfast love of God.

The hymn can be sung in several ways, according to local circumstances: 1) refrains by the congregation (people), verses by soloist as indicated in the music; 2) refrains by the choir, verses by a soloist; 3) sung in its entirety by a soloist. In cases 2 or 3, the refrain should be sung only once at the beginning and then after each verse. Metronome markings indicate the pace or tempo.

If the HYMN OF PRAISE is not sung, it may be read in unison by the congregation.

4. Suggested Old Testament readings for the First Lesson:[2]
   • Genesis 1:26-31
   Male and female created by God
   • Genesis 2:18-24
   God creates man and woman

[2] Two lessons may be used instead of three as indicated. It is suggested that one be from the Old Testament and one be from the New Testament.

- Song of Solomon 2:10-13

Love in the spring

- Song of Solomon 8:7

Unquenchable love

- Isaiah 63 :7-9

The steadfast love of God

5. Suggested psalms: 33, 100, 117, 127, 128, 136, 150. The psalm should be sung either by soloist, choir, congregation, or a combination of these. Various methods for singing psalms are available.[3] If the psalm is not sung, a hymn may be sung instead.

---

[3] Anglican Chant:

The Canadian Psalter, Anglican Church of Canada, Toronto

The Parish Psalter, Sydney Nicholson, Faith Press, London

Gelineau psalms:

(Several Collections are available), Gregorian Institute of America

Plainsong:

The Sunday Psalter, Herbert Lindemann and Newman Powell, Concordia Publishing House

Biblical Hymns and Psalms, Lucien Deiss, World Library of Sacred Music

Psalms for Singing, S. Somerville, World Library of Sacred Music

The Service Propers Noted, Paul Bunjes, Concordia Publishing House

6. Suggested Epistles for the Second Lesson:
   - Romans 12:1-2

   A living offering
   - 1 Corinthians 12:31-13:13

   The hymn of divine love
   - Ephesians 5:21-33

   Marriage and the church

7. The text of the ALLELUIA verse is 1 John 4:12. During Lent only the text itself is sung or said; the "alleluias" are omitted. They are also omitted if the ALLELUIA is read rather than sung.

   The musical setting is intended to be sung in its entirety by a soloist or choir in unison. Metronome markings indicate the pace or tempo.

8. Suggested Gospels:
   - Matthew 19:4-6

   Faithfulness in marriage
   - John 2:1-10

   The wedding at Cana

9. A brief, appropriate selection from a non-biblical writer, especially from a contem-

porary source, may be read before the sermon.

10. Suggested hymns:
   "Lord, who at Cana's wedding feast" (*SBH* 301, *TLH* 620)

   "Gracious Spirit, Holy Ghost" (*SBH* 119)

   "Deck thyself with joy and gladness" (*SBH* 262, *TLH* 305)

   "O perfect love" (*SBH* 300, *TLH* 623)

   "O Lord of love, whose truth" (*Worship Supplement* 781)

   "We are one in the Spirit" (Contemporary Worship 1: *Hymns*, 2)

   "Sons of God, hear his holy Word!" (CW 1: *Hymns*, 16)

   "Strong Son of God, immortal Love" (CW 1: *Hymns*, 17)

   "Our Father, by whose name all fatherhood is known" (CW 1: *Hymns*, 21)

11. The promises are the bride's and the groom's own, and provision should be made for those who want to write their own form of the promises, provided that they indicate the complete sharing which

marriage implies and make clear that the
promises are to be a life-long commitment.
For it is not a formula but the promise of
fidelity that makes a marriage.

12. The presiding minister places his hand
over the joined hands of the bride and
groom. It is customary in some places
for him first to bind their hands by laying
the end of his stole over them as a sign
of their union in God. Other signs of the
marriage that may be appropriate—
garlands or crowns—could be used.

13. If the parents have been standing behind
the bride and groom during the vows,
they lay their hands on the heads of their
children in blessing.

14. The words of the blessing are from Psalm
61:7. An alternate or additional verse is:
Let us rejoice and be glad for you;
let us praise your love more than wine,
   and your caresses more than any
   song.

Song of Solomon 1:4

15. Extending the sign of peace is especially appropriate at a wedding. The bride and groom should embrace. Others in the wedding party and in the congregation may clasp each other's hands and say, "Peace be with you," or another greeting more natural to them.

16. There should be silence after each bidding to pray. Other suitable prayers may be used. In Canadian churches where it is customary, the Register may be signed before the prayers begin.
    If there is no Communion, the service may conclude following the prayers with the OUR FATHER and benediction. This option may be used in creating a third form of the Marriage Service.

17. The offering of bread and wine is brought to the altar by the ushers or other representatives of the bridal party.

    The bread may be baked by a member of the bridal party, a friend, or a relative.

    Offerings of money need not be gathered at this service, but if they are, the offering should be given to some worthy cause designated by the bride and groom. The bride and groom may make an appropriate thank offering.

18. In place of the order for Holy Communion as outlined here from Contemporary Worship: *The Holy Communion,* either that in the *Service Book and Hymnal* or *The Lutheran Hymnal* may be used. Begin with the preface (*SBH* page 9, *TLH* page 24).

19. The Great Thanksgiving in Contemporary Worship: *The Holy Communion,* pages 15-17, or any other appropriate eucharistic prayer may be used.

20. Under no circumstances shall the bride and groom receive the sacrament to the exclusion of the congregation. The meal is for the assembled family of God.

21. Suggested hymns after Communion:
      "Now thank we all our God" (*SBH* 443, *TLH* 36)

"Come with us, O blessed Jesus" (*SBH* 283)

"Jerusalem the golden" (*SBH* 584, *TLH* 613)

22. The wedding party may leave the church during a hymn, suitable instrumental music, or in silence.
The wedding reception can be understood as an extension of the banquet already shared in the Lord's Supper.

23. The lessons from the Bible for A Second Form of The Marriage Service are to be selected from the suggested readings listed under notes 4, 6, and 8 above.

The Presbyterian Service*

ORDER FOR THE
PUBLIC WORSHIP OF GOD

THE MARRIAGE SERVICE

The man and the woman to be married may be seated together facing the Lord's

* From *The Worshipbook*. Copyright © MCMLXX, MCMLXXII, The Westminster Press. Used by permission.

table, with their families, friends, and members of the congregation seated with them.

When the people have assembled, let the minister say:

Let us worship God.

There was a marriage at Cana in Galilee; Jesus was invited to the marriage, with his disciples.

Friends: Marriage is established by God. In marriage a man and a woman willingly bind themselves together in love, and become one even as Christ is one with the church, his body.

Let marriage be held in honor among all.

All may join in a hymn of praise and the following prayer:

Let us confess our sin before God.

Almighty God, our Father: you created us for life together. We confess that we have turned from your will. We have not loved one another as you commanded. We have been quick to claim our own rights and careless of the rights of others. We have taken much and given little. Forgive our disobedience, O God, and strengthen us in

love, so that we may serve you as a faithful people, and live together in your joy; through Jesus Christ our Lord. Amen.

The minister shall declare God's mercy, saying:

Hear and believe the good news of the gospel.

Nothing can separate us from the love of God in Christ Jesus our Lord!

In Jesus Christ, we are forgiven.

The people may stand to sing a doxology, or some other appropriate response to the good mercy of God.

The minister may offer a Prayer for Illumination.

Before the reading of the Old Testament lesson, the minister shall say:

The lesson is . . .

Listen for the word of God.

The Gloria Patri, or some other response, may be sung.

Before the reading of the New Testament lesson, the minister shall say:

The lesson is . . .

Listen for the word of God.

The minister may deliver a brief Sermon on the lessons from Scripture, concluding with an Ascription of Praise.

Then let the minister address the man and woman, saying:

_____ and _____, you have come together according to God's wonderful plan for creation. Now, before these people, say your vows to each other.

Let the man and the woman stand before the people, facing each other. Then, the minister shall say:

Be subject to one another out of reverence for Christ.

The man shall say to the woman:

_____, I promise with God's help to be your faithful husband, to love and serve you as Christ commands, as long as we both shall live.

The woman shall say to the man:

_____, I promise with God's help to be your faithful wife, to love and serve you as Christ commands, as long as we both shall live.

A ring, or rings, may be given, with the

following words:

I give you this ring as a sign of my promise.

The minister shall address the man and the woman, saying:

As God's picked representatives of the new humanity, purified and beloved of God himself, be merciful in action, kindly in heart, humble in mind. Accept life, and be most patient and tolerant with one another. Forgive as freely as the Lord has forgiven you. And, above everything else, be truly loving. Let the peace of Christ rule in your hearts, remembering that as members of the one body you are called to live in harmony, and never forget to be thankful for what God has done for you.

Or,

Love is slow to lose patience—it looks for a way of being constructive. It is not possessive: it is neither anxious to impress nor does it cherish inflated ideas of its own importance. Love has good manners and does not pursue selfish advantage. It is not touchy. It does not keep account of evil or gloat over the wickedness of other people. On the contrary, it is glad with all good men when truth pre-

vails. Love knows no limit to its endurance, no
end to its trust, no fading of its hope; it can
outlast anything. It still stands when all else
has fallen.

The minister shall call the people to prayer,
saying:

Praise the Lord.

The Lord's name be praised.

Lift up your hearts.

We lift them to the Lord.

Let us pray.

Eternal God: without your grace no promise
is sure. Strengthen _____ and _____ with
the gift of your Spirit, so they may fulfill the
vows they have taken. Keep them faithful to
each other and to you. Fill them with such
love and joy that they may build a home where
no one is a stranger. And guide them by your
word to serve you all the days of their lives;
through Jesus Christ our Lord, to whom be
honor and glory forever and ever. **Amen.**

The Lord's Prayer shall be said.

Then, the man and the woman having
joined hands, the minister shall say:

_____ and _____, you are now husband

and wife according to the witness of the holy catholic church, and the law of the state. Become one. Fulfill your promises. Love and serve the Lord.

What God has united, man must not divide.

Here may be sung a hymn of thanksgiving. Then, let the people be dismissed:

Glory be to him who can keep you from falling and bring you safe to his glorious presence, innocent and happy. To God, the only God, who saves us through Jesus Christ our Lord, be the glory, majesty, authority, and power, which he had before time began, now and forever. **Amen.**

Or,

The grace of the Lord Jesus Christ, the love of God, and the fellowship of the Holy Spirit, be with you all. **Amen.**

ORDER FOR THE PUBLIC WORSHIP OF GOD

A Service for the Recognition of a Marriage

This service may be used to recognize a

civil marriage; or with the deletion of the first paragraph, it may be used as a brief marriage service.

The service may be conducted during public worship on the Lord's Day, when the Sacrament is not celebrated, immediately after the preaching of a sermon; or it may be used at other times. Members of the congregation should be present, in addition to the minister.

Let the minister or an elder say:

_____ and _____ have been married by the law of the state, and they have spoken vows pledging loyalty and love. Now, in faith, they come before the witness of the church to acknowledge their marriage covenant and to tell their common purpose in the Lord.

Then, the minister shall say:

Friends: Marriage is God's gift. In marriage a man and a woman bind themselves in love and become one, even as Christ is one with the church, his body.

_____ and _____, be subject to one another out of reverence for Christ.

The man shall say to the woman:

_____, *you are my wife. With God's help I promise to be your faithful husband, to love and serve you as Christ commands, as long as we both shall live.*

The woman shall say to the man:

_____, *you are my husband. With God's help I promise to be your faithful wife, to love and serve you as Christ commands, as long as we both shall live.*

A ring, or rings, may be given, with the following words:

I give you this ring as a sign of my promise.

Then, let the minister say:

Hear the words of our Lord Jesus Christ: Remain in my love. If you keep my commandments you will remain in my love, just as I have kept my Father's commandments and remain in his love. I have told you this so that my own joy may be in you and your joy be complete. This is my commandment: love one another, as I have loved you.

Let us pray.

Eternal God: without your grace no promise is sure. Strengthen _____ and _____ with the gift of your Spirit, so they may fulfill the vows they have taken. Keep them faithful to each other and to you. Fill them with such love and joy that they may build a home where no one is a stranger. And guide them by your word to serve you all the days of their lives; through Jesus Christ our Lord, to whom be honor and glory, forever and ever. **Amen.**

The man and the woman having joined hands, the minister shall say:

_____ and _____, you are husband and wife according to the witness of the holy catholic church. Help each other. Be united; live in peace, and the God of love and peace will be with you.

What God has united, man must not divide.

The following benediction may be said:

The grace of the Lord Jesus Christ, the love of God, and the fellowship of the Holy Spirit, be with you all. **Amen.**

A "FREE" SERVICE
FOR WEDDINGS*

The Prelude**

    "Kum Ba Yah"—African (Angola)

    "The Gift of Love"—Hal Hopson

    "Entreat Me Not"—Words based on Ruth
        1:16, 17, and Music by James Oosting

The Processional

    "Ode to Joy" **—Beethoven

    Sutherlin—(words by Nancy) Sung by
        congregation, standing)

This is the saddest and gladdest of times,
when sadness is sweet and gladness is sober.
Something dies today, and something is born.

---

  * Used with the permission of the author, Dr. John
Killinger, Professor of Preaching, the Divinity School,
Vanderbilt University (1973).

  ** From *Folk Songs for Weddings* (Carol Stream,
Ill.: Hope Publishing Co., 1972).

  Music may employ voices, guitars, and other suitable
instruments available according to preference.

The past becomes past; the future reaches out.
This is a time between the times, a time without time, a moment that will exist for its own
sake, for the sake of what we do here. It is,
in other words, a holy moment, a sacred moment, a transcendent moment.

We are here to celebrate.

What we bring with us is mainly who we
are and what we have been. Memories crowd
upon the parents: of innocence and experience, of childhood and beyond. The softness
of baby flesh after a bath . . . the inarticulate
sounds of a voice not yet tuned to speech . . .
the first step . . . the first accident . . . the
first Christmas . . . the first birthday . . . first
day at school . . . first part on a program . . .
first date . . . first job . . . Maybe children
are *made* of memories.

And through it all, the real desire in the
hearts of the parents was that these children
should learn to love . . . to give love and receive it . . . not just for the things they wanted
and needed, as a commodity, but genuinely,
deeply, with their whole beings.

Now we are at a special moment in that development toward love when these particular children, (*Bride*) and (*Groom*), feeling incomplete alone, have discovered that something special in them, something about the way they are made, enables them to find more fulfillment together than they could have hoped to find apart. And, having discovered this, they wish to sanctify this union, to give it a unique meaning and significance, by celebrating it here, in your presence, in a church.

What lies ahead is not certain. It never is. They are human beings, and, therefore, the patterns of their growth and development are not wholly predictable. But they have reached a new time in their lives today, a time for tying a knot in the rope of days and saying, "We will not slip backwards here. Now we are going forward." It is a time for taking vows, for facing the uncertainties with the things about which they are certain, namely, that they love each other and that whatever the future brings they will face it together.

We are here to witness this event, and to celebrate it with them. They don't have to have us. Love does its own thing. But they have chosen to share this time with us, and perhaps to derive some strength and assurance, in future days, from our having been here when they took this step.

Their parents are here, of course, and their friends—the persons who have nurtured and shaped and helped to bring them to this hour. I am sure they would want me to express to you, in this exciting moment for them, their sense of gratitude for the part of you that has gone into their lives and consequently into this moment. They are what they are, and will become what they will become, in some measure because of you.

Now you realize, as well as I, that this makes you responsible for them in the future. There is an Oriental proverb which says that anyone who saves a man's life is thereafter responsible for it. It is reasonable also to expect that anyone who gives something of himself to the shaping of another person's life is thereafter responsible for the destiny of that life.

So this is our time too, not just theirs. We have our vows to make too, as well as they. By just being here, we are involved with them and their future. When they laugh, it is ours to laugh with them. When they cry, it is ours to weep. And when they hurt, it is ours to give comfort. It is a dangerous thing to attend a wedding.

The father of the bride stands here to give the bride away, as we have always said. He stands here for his wife too, and for the bride's brothers, and for all of you. He makes the gift in your behalf.

Who gives this woman to be wed to this man?

"Her mother and I do."

The man, it is always assumed, gives himself away. But no mother or father here can really believe that that is so, for you know the heart of a mother and father, and what is taking place inside Mr. and Mrs. _____ right now—the mingled joy and pain at seeing their son reach this new point in life, and assume this new role of responsibility and manhood. In their case, it is a matter of giving away something of themselves, in order that the common joy may be served.

[At the altar]

Now we focus on the bride and groom themselves. They are nervous, and that is good. They have never made such an important commitment before. They can sense the wildness and grandeur and beauty and danger of what they are doing. They do not do it lightly.

(*Bride*), this is a very, very important important moment. You are sealing, in one large instance, innumerable small commitments you have made. The past has delivered you to this occasion, and you are pledging all of it to this union. Do you have a ring?

When you put this ring on (*Groom's*) hand, it becomes a symbol of your gift of self. Your ability to give yourself to him is not perfect now; but you will learn to give yourself more and more until the gift is like the ring, continuous and whole.

Do you pledge yourself to this?

"I do."

(*Groom*), you are taking on a man's world now, and a man's full role in that world. You may have thought things were hard at various times of your life; you may find them even harder now. But you will also find strength and comfort against the hardness, for you will not be alone now.

Do you have a ring?

When you put this ring on (*Bride's*) finger, it becomes a symbol of your pledge to her, and to all of us here, that you are going to encircle her with your love, your care, and your protection; that, whatever happens, she can depend on you. We do not expect you to know all that that means now; but we do expect that you are pledging your will, so that, whatever turns there are in the road ahead, we may depend upon your being there with her, supporting her with your very life.

Do you pledge yourself to this?

[I do.]

It is done. Now what about us? Shall we signify to this couple what the vow-taking means to us? Are we ready to commit ourselves to them, to love them, to seek their best interest at all times, to encourage them in all circumstances, now and in the future?

Say, "We are."

Then the moment is almost complete. There is only one thing remaining. It should be set into the perspective of the holy occasion it is. Let us do that now. Let us pray.

Our Father, who sanctions marriage, as you approve all acts and efforts of men to come together more perfectly, give your blessings now to what we have done here. Make the moment fruitful to this couple in terms of added devotion, of new inner strength, and of a new sense of the sacredness of all life. We do not ask that they be kept from sorrow and trial, but that they may learn from these, and be stronger because of them. We do not ask that all life be easy and profitable to them, but that they find it good and worth celebrating. We hope they will have children, as further objects of their love, and that they will find all their tasks in life, including the task of being human, easier because they approach those tasks together. Make them each quick to forgive, quick to laugh, quick to enjoy, and quick to see the worth of each other. Let each so value the personality of the other that he may not wish to alter it into some other course, but to exalt it, to draw it out, to adore it. And let them, in the measure of time that is theirs together, find much joy in many small things. Through Jesus Christ our Lord, who has taught us, when we pray together, to ask simply,

(Congregation prays)

Our Father, who art in heaven, hallowed be thy name. Thy kingdom come, thy will be done, on earth as it is in heaven. Give us this day our daily bread, and forgive us our trespasses as we forgive those who trespass against us. And lead us not into temptation, but deliver us from evil. For thine is the kingdom, and the power, and the glory, forever. Amen.

And now, _____ and _____, it is really done. You are man and wife. In our eyes at least. It will take you a long time really to grow into the meaning of that. But you are on your way, and with our blessings.

THE CELEBRATION OF THE LORD'S SUPPER

Having made these commitments, we shall appropriate the symbols of the Christian tradition for our celebration. (Minister explains procedure)*

Before we participate in this celebration, let us remind ourselves of its significance. We shall drink the wine and eat the bread which are symbols for the brokenness of Jesus who is everyman. Let us affirm our brokenness as

---

* Each minister plans the celebration according to his denomination's liturgy and in consultation with the couple.

togetherness! We shall serve and be served as gestures symbolic of Jesus' giving his life away to give us new lives as possibilities. Let us understand that as we serve this bread and wine we are deciding to give our lives away and accept the lives of others as we seek to love and to establish peace. So let us celebrate our brokenness as togetherness, and let us decide for love and peace!

"Let Us Break Bread Together"**—Spiritual (Arr. by John F. Wilson)

Distribution of the Elements

Passing of the Peace ("The Lord be with you"; reponse: "And with you, _____.")
The Recessional—"They'll Know We Are Christians By Our Love"**—Congregation

The Benediction

** From *Folk Songs for Weddings* (Carol Stream, Ill.: Hope Publishing Co., 1972).

PART III

STATE LAWS REGARDING MARRIAGE

Note: In June, 1967, the United States Supreme Court in *Loving v. Commonwealth of Virginia,* 388 U.S. 1, held the Virginia miscegenation statute, and *inferentially all other miscegenation statutes,* to be in violation of the Equal Protection Clause of the Fourteenth Amendment to the United States Constitution.

The opinion of Mr. Chief Justice Warren for a unanimous court took the broad position that, "There can be no doubt that restricting the freedom to marry solely because of racial classifications violates the central meaning of the Equal Protection Clause. . . . These statutes also deprive the Lovings of Liberty without due process of law in violation of the Due Process Clause of the Fourteenth Amendment."

(87 Sup. Ct. at 1823, 1824)

In light of the Supreme Court decision in *Loving v. Commonwealth of Virginia,* those state statutes dealing with miscegenation have been deemed unconstitutional. An asterisk (*) will be used to designate those states that incorporated or still incorporate statutes of this type.

Alabama*

License issued by probate judge of county in which the woman resides or in which ceremony is to be performed. Cost of license, $2.00. Minimum ages: male, 17; female, 14. Parental consent necessary when male is under 21, female under 18. No marriage of male venereals. Blood test required. Man is not permitted to marry mother, daughter, granddaughter, sister, half-sister, aunt, niece, half-niece, stepmother, son's widow, stepdaughter, or wife's granddaughter.

Alaska

Cost of license, $5.00. Waiting period for license, 3 days. No waiting period necessary after issuance. Minimum ages: male, 18; female, 16. Parental consent necessary when male is under 19, female under 18. Blood test required.

Arizona

License issued by clerk of superior court in county in which one of the parties resides or in which marriage is to take place. Cost of license, $5.00. Minimum ages: male, 18; female, 16. Parental consent necessary when male is under 21, female under 18. Blood test required. Man is not permitted to marry mother, daughter, grandmother, granddaughter, sister, aunt, niece, first cousin.

Arkansas

License issued by clerk of county court in any county. Waiting period for license, 3 days. Minimum ages: male, 18; female, 16. Parental consent necessary when male is under 21, female under 18. Cost of license, $1.50. Minister must record license/credentials with county clerk. Prohibited degrees of relationship: all marriages between parents and children, grandparents and grandchildren of every degree, brothers and sisters of half and whole blood, uncles and nieces, aunts and nephews, first cousins.

California*

License issued by a county clerk of any county. Cost of license, $5.00. Parental consent necessary when male under 21, female under 18. Both parental consent and order of superior court required when male under 18, female under 16. Blood test required. Prohibited degrees of relationship: parents and children, ancestors and decendants of every degree, uncles and nieces, aunts and nephews, brothers and sisters of half and whole blood.

Colorado

License issued by any county clerk. Cost of license, $5.00. Minimum ages: male, 16; female, 16. Parental consent necessary if male is under 21, female under 18. Blood test required. Marriage between parents and children, grandparents and grandchildren of every degree, between brothers and sisters of half/whole blood, between uncles and nieces, aunts and nephews, are declared void.

Connecticut

License issued by registrar of births, marriages, and deaths of town in which marriage is to be celebrated. Waiting period for license, 5 days. Minimum ages: both sexes, 16 years. Parental consent necessary when under 21. Blood test required. Man may not marry mother, daughter, grandmother, granddaughter, sister, aunt, niece, stepmother, stepdaughter. Cost of license, $5.00.

Delaware*

License issued by Clerks of the Peace. Cost of license, $3.00. Waiting period for license, 1 day if one or both are residents, 4 days if both are nonresidents. Minimum ages: male, 18; female, 16. Parental consent necessary if male is under 19, female under 19. No marriage between person and his ancestor, descendant, brother, sister, uncle, aunt, niece, nephew, first cousin. No marriage if either party is epileptic, insane, venereally diseased, habitual drunkard, addict to narcotics, on probation/ parole unless proper filing, divorcee unless proper filing, pauper.

District of Columbia

License issued by the clerk's office of supreme court of the District of Columbia. Cost of the license, $0.50 on application; $2.00 when license is issued. Waiting period for license, 3 days. Minimum ages: male, 18; female, 16. Parental consent necessary when male is under 21, female under 18. Minister must be authorized by a justice of the supreme court of the district. No marriage of idiot or lunatic. Man cannot marry mother, daughter, grandmother, granddaughter, sister, aunt, niece, stepmother, daughter-in-law, grandfather's wife, grandson's

wife, mother-in-law, stepdaughter, wife's grandmother, wife's granddaughter.

Florida

License issued by judge of county in which
woman resides. Cost of license, $2.00 and addi-
tional $3.00 charge. Waiting period for license,
3 days. Minimum ages: male, 18; female, 16.
Parental consent necessary when under 21.
Blood test required. Man cannot marry mother,
daughter, grandmother, granddaughter, sister,
aunt, niece.

Georgia*

License issued by Ordinary of county where
female resides. If she is nonresident, by Ordinary of county where ceremony is to be performed. Cost of license, $5.00. Waiting period
for license, 3 days for parties who have passed
their 19th birthday but are not 21 years of
age. Parties 21 or older can obtain a marriage
license immediately upon application therefor.
Parties who have passed their 19th birthday
but are not yet 21 years of age may marry without consent, but must wait the mandatory 3-day
period. Parties 19 years of age and younger
must have the consent of parent or guardian
personally appearing before the Ordinary.

Blood test required. Man cannot marry mother, daughter, grandmother, granddaughter, sister, aunt, niece, stepmother, daughter-in-law, mother-in-law, stepdaughter, wife's granddaughter.

Hawaii

Cost of license, $5.00. No waiting period for license. Minimum ages: male, 18; female, 16. Parental consent necessary when male is under 20 and female under 18. Examination and blood test required. Prohibited relationships: parties related as ancestor and descendant to any degree, brother and sister of whole/half blood, uncle and niece, aunt and nephew. No marriage if either party is impotent or physically incapable, consent obtained by fraud/force, either party has leprosy or loathsome disease concealed from other party.

Idaho

License issued by county recorder of any county. Cost of license, $4.75. Waiting period for license, 3 days. Parental consent necessary when either party is under 18 but over 16 years old. When either party is under 16, both parental consent and court order necessary. Prohibited relationships and other reasons for voiding marriage: physical incapacity, marriage by fraud/force, marriage between parents and descendants of every degree, brothers and sisters of half or whole blood, uncles and nieces, aunts and nephews, first cousins, polygamous marriages. Blood test required.

Illinois

License issued by county clerk of county where marriage is to be solemnized (term "county clerk" interchangeable with "clerk of county court"). Members of the Society of Friends are exempted from this provision. Cost of license: for counties of the first and second class, $5.00; for counties of the third class, $10.00. Minimum ages: male, 16; female, 15. Parental consent necessary when male is under 21, female under 18. No marriages of the insane or idiots. Man may not marry mother, daughter, grandmother, granddaughter, sister, half-sister, aunt, niece, grandaunt, great-grandaunt, first cousin.

Indiana

License issued by the clerk of circuit court of county in which either party resides. Cost of license, $3.00. Waiting period for license, 3 days. Members of the Society of Friends are exempted from the necessity of license. Minimum ages: male, 18; female, 16. Parental consent necessary when male is under 21, female under 18. Blood test required. No marriage of imbeciles, epileptics, insane, narcotic addicts, drunkards, or those suffering from transmissible disease. Man may not marry mother, daughter, grandmother, granddaughter, sister, aunt, niece, grandaunt, great-grandaunt, first cousin, grandniece, first cousin once removed.

Iowa

License issued by clerk of district court of county where marriage will be solemnized. Cost of license, $3.00. Minimum ages: male, 18; female, 16. Parental consent necessary when male is under 21, female under 18. Blood test required. No marriage of imbeciles, insane. Waiting period for license, 3 days. Man may not marry mother, daughter, grandmother, granddaughter, sister, aunt, niece, first cousin, stepmother, son's widow, grandson's widow, mother-in-law, stepdaughter.

Kansas

License issued by probate judge of any county. Cost of license, $5.00 (includes $1.00 registration fee). Waiting period for license, 3 days. Minimum ages: male, 18; female, 18. Parental consent and consent of probate judge necessary when male is under 18, female under 18. Blood test required. No marriage if incapacitated unless woman is over forty-five. Man may not marry mother, daughter, grandmother, granddaughter, sister, half-sister, aunt, niece, first cousin.

Kentucky*

License issued by clerk of county in which female resides. Cost of license, $3.50. Waiting period for license, 3 days. Parental consent necessary when male under 18, female under 16. Blood test required. Minister must obtain license from court of county in which he resides. Two witnesses required. No marriage of idiots or insane. Man may not marry mother, daughter, grandmother, granddaughter, sister, aunt, niece, grandniece, stepmother, stepdaughter, grandfather's wife, grandson's wife, mother-in-law, daughter-in-law, wife's grandmother, wife's granddaughter.

Louisiana*

License issued in New Orleans by board of health and judges of city courts; in other parishes by clerks of courts. Cost of license, $2.00. Waiting period of 72 hours after license is issued. Minimum ages: male, 18; female, 16. Parental consent necessary when under 21. Three witnesses required. Man may not marry mother, daughter, grandmother, granddaughter, sister, half-sister, aunt, niece, first cousin.

Maine

License issued by clerk of town in which one or both parties reside. If both parties are non-residents of state, license issued by clerk of town in which ceremony to be solemnized. Waiting period for license, 5 days. Two witnesses required. Parental consent required if female or male under 18. If either party under 16, both parental consent and consent of county probate judge required. Minister must be licensed by the state. Prohibited relationships: man may not marry mother, grandmother, daughter, stepmother, grandfather's wife, son's wife, grandson's wife, wife's mother, wife's grandmother, wife's daughter, wife's granddaughter, sister, brother's daughter, sister's daughter, father's sister, mother's sister. Cost of license, $6.00.

Maryland

License to be issued by clerk of circuit court for county in which marriage is to be performed; if in Baltimore City, from clerk of Court of Common Pleas. Waiting time for license, 48 hours. Cost of license, $2.00 (exceptions should be noted). Minimum ages: male, 18; female, 16 unless showing pregnancy. Parental consent necessary if male over 18 but under 21, female over 16 but under 18. Man may not marry: grandmother, grandfather's wife, wife's grandmother, father's sister, mother's sister, mother, stepmother, wife's mother, daughter, wife's daughter, son's wife, sister, son's daughter, daughter's daughter, son's son's wife, daughter's son's wife, wife's son's daughter, wife's daughter's daughter, brother's daughter, sister's daughter.

Massachusetts

License issued by clerk of city or town where parties reside. If only one is a resident, then by clerk of place of residence. If neither are residents, by clerk of any city or town. Intention to marry must be filed with the clerk. Three day waiting period between filing the notice of intention and the issuance of the license. Premarital blood test required. Cost of

license: $2.00 for residents; $4.00 for nonresidents. Parental consent required if female
between 16 and 18 years of age. If female is
under 16 and male under 18, a court order is
necessary. Divorced person may remarry after
the decree becomes absolute which is after ex-
piration of six months from the entry of decree
nisi. Man may not marry mother, daughter,
grandmother, granddaughter, sister, aunt,
niece, stepmother, daughter-in-law, grandfather's wife, mother-in-law, stepdaughter,
wife's granddaughter. Insane persons incapable
of contracting marriage.

Michigan

License issued by county clerk of county in
which either party lives; if nonresident, in
county in which ceremony is to be solemnized.
Cost of license, $5.00 for residents, $15.00 for
nonresidents. Waiting period for license, 3
days. Minimum ages: male, 18; female, 16.
Parental consent necessary when under 18.
Blood test required. Two witnesses required.
Marriage of venereals, idiots, or insane not
permitted. Man may not marry mother, daughter, grandmother, granddaughter, sister, aunt,
niece, stepmother, daughter-in-law, stepdaughter, wife's grandmother, wife's granddaughter,

or cousin of the first degree. Women: Same as for male regarding relations.

Minnesota

License issued by clerk of district court of county in which woman resides; if nonresident, from clerk of court any location. Cost of license, $3.00. Waiting period for license, 5 days. Minimum ages: Every male who is 21, every female who is 18 is capable of marriage. Male 18 years old and female 16 years of age with the consent of the parents, guardian, or juvenile court of county in which they live. No blood test required. Ministers must have certificate from clerk of district court of some county in the state. Two witnesses required. No marriage of feeble-minded or insane. Marriages between persons of nearer of kin than second cousins prohibited.

Mississippi*

License issued by clerk of circuit court of county in which female usually resides. Cost of license, $5.00. Waiting period for license, 3 days. Minimum ages: male, 17; female, 15. Parental consent necessary when male is under 21, female under 18. Blood test required. No marriage of insane or idiots. Man may not marry mother, daughter, grandmother, granddaughter, sister, half-sister, aunt, niece, first cousin, stepmother, son's widow, stepdaughter, wife's granddaughter.

Missouri

License issued by county recorder, or recorder of the city of St. Louis. Cost of license, $2.55. Waiting period for license, 3 days. Minimum ages: male, 15; female, 15. Parental consent necessary when male is under 21, female under 18. Blood test required. No marriage of insane, imbecile, feebleminded, or epileptic. Man may not marry mother, daughter, grandmother, granddaughter, sister, half-sister, aunt, niece, first cousin. Statute prohibits marriage between grandparents and grandchildren of every degree.

Montana

License issued by clerk of district court of county in which one of the parties has resided for at least five days if Montana residents; may be used in any county in the state. Nonresidents obtain license from clerk of district court in county in which ceremony will take

place. Cost of license, $5.00. Five days wait-
ing period; provision for waiver provided. Minimum ages: male, 19; female, 19 (no minimum
age if permission of parents or guardians and
consent of district judge is obtained). Blood
test is required. No marriage of the feeble-
minded. Man may not marry mother, daughter,
grandmother, granddaughter, sister, half-sister,
aunt, niece, first cousin. Statute prohibits marriage between ancestors and descendants.

Nebraska

License issued by any county judge, marriage
may be performed in any other county. Cost
of license, $5.00. Minimum ages: male, 18;
female, 16. Parental consent necessary when
either party is under age 20. Blood tests required. Man may not marry mother, daughter,
grandmother, granddaughter, sister, aunt,
niece, first cousin. Five day waiting period between application for license and the time
license can be issued.

Nevada

License issued by clerk of any county in the
state. Cost of license, $5.00. Minimum ages:
male, 18; female, 16. Parental consent necessary when male is under 21, female under 18.

No blood test required. Ministerial license necessary. Two witnesses required. No marriage of venereals, insane, or idiots. Man may not marry mother, daughter, grandmother, granddaughter, sister, aunt, niece, grandaunt, great-grandaunt, first cousin, first cousin once removed, or anyone of closer kin than second cousin.

New Hampshire

Certificate of intention must be filed with clerk of city or town in which either party resides; if nonresidents, with clerk of city or town in which marriage is to be solemnized. Cost of license, $3.00. Waiting period of license, 5 days. Minimum ages: male, 14; female, 13. Parental consent necessary when male is under 20, female under 18. Blood test required. No marriage of imbeciles, feeble-minded, idiots, or insane. Man may not marry father's sister, mother's sister, father's widow, wife's mother, daughter, wife's daughter, son's widow, sister, son's daughter, daughter's daughter, son's son's widow, daughter's son's widow, brother's daughter, or sister's daughter, father's brother's daughter, mother's brother's daughter, father's sister's daughter, or mother's sister's daughter. No woman may marry her father, father's brother, mother's brother, mother's husband,

husband's father, son, husband's son, daughter's husband, brother, son's son, daughter's son, son's daughter's husband, daughter's daughter's husband, brother's son, sister's son, father's brother's son, mother's brother's son, father's sister's son or mother's sister's son.

New Jersey

License issued in first-class cities by clerk of city; elsewhere by registrar of vital statistics. If there be no registrar of vital statistics, by clerk of the municipality or assessor of taxes or their deputies. Cost of license, $3.00. Waiting period for license, 72 hours. It shall be issued in the municipality in which the man lives; if both are nonresidents, in the municipality in which the marriage is to take place. Minimum ages: both parental consents and judicial approval of such consents are necessary if the male is under 18 or the female is under 16. Consent of both parents necessary if the male is under 21 or the female is under 16. Blood test required. Two witnesses necessary. No marriage of venereals, narcotics, imbeciles, epileptics, or insane. Man may not marry mother, daughter, grandmother, granddaughter, sister, half-sister, niece, half-niece, aunt, half-aunt. Marriage between ancestors and descendants prohibited.

New Mexico

License issued by county clerk of county in which marriage will take place. Cost of license, $5.00. Minimum ages: male, 18; female, 16. Parental consent necessary when male is under 18, female under 18. Blood test required. Man may not marry mother, daughter, grandmother, granddaughter, sister, half-sister, aunt, niece. Marriage between grandparents and grandchildren of every degree prohibited. Cousins may marry. Seventy-two hour waiting period between application and issuance of license. This requirement may be waived by district judge or magistrate.

New York

License issued by town or city clerk. Waiting period for license, 1 day. Cost of license, $2.00. Minimum ages: male, 16; female, 14. Blood test required. Prohibited relationships: marriage is void between ancestor and descendant, brother and sister of half/whole blood, uncle and niece, aunt and nephew. Every person authorized to perform marriage in New York City must register with city clerk.

North Carolina

License issued by registrar of deeds of county in which marriage is to take place. Cost of license, $5.00. Minimum age: 16 for both sexes. Parental consent necessary when under 18. Health certificate and blood test required. Two or more witnesses. No marriage of venereals or mental incompetents. Insane person permitted to marry after eugenic sterilization. No marriage of those afflicted with tuberculosis in the infectious stages. Persons of nearer kin than first cousins or double first cousins may not marry.

North Dakota

License issued by judge of county in which either party resides. If that county be unorganized, then by the county to which it is attached for judicial purposes. No marriage of nonresidents. Cost of license, $1.00. Minimum ages: male, 18; female, 15. Parental consent necessary when male is under 21, female under 18. Blood test required. No marriage of drunkards, imbeciles, criminals, idiots, feeble-minded, or insane, except when woman is over forty-five. Man may not marry mother, daughter, grandmother, granddaughter, sister, half-sister, aunt, niece, first cousin, half-first cousin. Marriage between grandparents and grandchildren of every degree prohibited.

Ohio

License issued by probate judge of county in which woman resides. Waiting period for license, 5 days. No marriage of nonresidents. Minimum ages: male, 18; female, 16. Parental consent necessary when under 21. Blood test required. Minister must obtain a license from probate judge of the county before he can officiate ceremony. No marriage of habitual drunkards, epileptics, narcotics, imbeciles, or insane. Man may not marry mother, daughter, grandmother, granddaughter, sister, aunt, niece, grandaunt, great-grandaunt, first cousin, grandniece, great grandniece, first cousin once removed. Cost of license, $2.50.

Oklahoma

License issued by judge or clerk of county court of county in which marriage is to be solemnized. Cost of license, $3.00. Minimum ages: male 18; female, 15. Parental consent necessary when male is under 21, female under 18. Blood test required. Minister must file credentials with judge of the county. Two witnesses necessary. Man may not marry mother, daughter, grandmother, stepmother, stepdaughter. Marriage between ancestors and descendants of any degree prohibited.

Oregon

License issued by clerk of any county. Cost of license, $10.00. Waiting period for license, 7 days. Minimum ages: male, 18; female, 15. Parental consent necessary when male is under 21, female under 18. Blood test required. Clergyman must file credentials with county clerk. Two witnesses required. Man may not marry mother, daughter, granddaughter, sister, half-sister, aunt, half-aunt, niece, half-niece, first cousin, half-first cousin.

Pennsylvania

License issued by clerk of orphans' court of county in which marriage to take place. Cost of license, $2.50. Waiting period for license, 3 days. Residence time, 1 year. Blood test required. Minimum ages: 16 for both parties unless judge of orphans' court decides it in best interest. Parental consent necessary when either party is under 18. No marriage if either party is weak-minded, insane, or of unsound mind. Prohibited relationships: man may not marry mother, father's sister, mother's sister, sister, daughter, daughter of son/daughter, first cousin, father's wife, son's wife, wife's daughter, daughter of wife's son/daughter.

Rhode Island

License issued by clerk of town or city in which either party resides; if nonresidents, town or city in which ceremony will be performed. Cost of license, $2.00. Waiting period, 5 days if the bride is a nonresident. No waiting period for marriage license if the bride is a resident of the city or town within the state. Minimum ages: male, 18; female, 16. Parental consent necessary when under 21. Blood test required. Clergymen must secure license from clerk of town or city. Two witnesses required for ceremony. No marriage of lunatics. Man may not marry mother, sister, daughter, grandmother, granddaughter, aunt, niece, stepmother, daughter-in-law, grandfather's wife, grandson's wife, mother-in-law, stepdaughter, wife's grandmother, wife's granddaughter.

South Carolina

License issued by judge of probate court. Cost of license, $1.00. Waiting period for license, 24 hours. Minimum ages: male, 16; female, 16 where license cannot be issued even with consent of the parent or guardian. If male between ages of 16 and 18 and the female is between 14 and 18, a license cannot be issued without the consent of parent, guardian, or relative with whom the party lives. No blood test required. Idiots and lunatics may not marry. Man may not marry mother, daughter, grandmother, granddaughter, sister, aunt, niece, stepmother, son's wife, grandfather's wife, grandson's wife, wife's mother, stepdaughter, wife's grandmother, wife's granddaughter.

South Dakota

License issued by clerk of court of county in which marriage is to take place. Minimum ages: male, 18; female, 16. Parental consent necessary when male is under 21, female under 18. Blood test required. Two witnesses necessary. Man may not marry mother, daughter, grandmother, granddaughter, sister, half-sister, aunt, niece, first cousin, half-first cousin, son's wife. No marriage between ancestors and descendants. Cost of license: $5.00.

Tennessee*

License issued by clerk of county court of county where female resides or where marriage is to be solemnized. Cost of license, $8.00. Waiting period for license, 3 days. Minimum ages: 16 for both sexes. Written parental consent necessary when under 18. Blood test required. Those of unsound mind may not marry. Man may not marry mother, daughter, grandmother, granddaughter, sister, half-sister, aunt, niece, half-niece, grandniece, half-grandniece, great-grandniece, stepmother, son's wife, grandson's wife, stepdaughter, wife's granddaughter, any lineal descendant of a spouse, spouse of any lineal descendant.

Texas

License issued by county clerk of any county. Minimum ages: male, 16; female, 14. Parental consent necessary if male is under 19, female under 18. Blood test required. Cost of license, $.50. Prohibited relationships: ancestor and descendant by blood or adoption, brother and sister of half/whole blood or by adoption, parent's brother or sister of half/whole blood. Marriage voidable if either party is underage, impotent, under influence of alcohol/narcotics at time of marriage, marriage by fraud/force, mentally incompetent, concealed divorce within 6 months of marriage, death.

Utah*

License issued by clerk of county in which woman resides unless she be 18 years or older, or a widow, in which case it may be issued in any county upon written application. Cost of license, $5.00. Minimum ages: male, 16; female, 14. Parental consent necessary when male is under 21, female under 18. Blood test required. Two witnesses necessary. Man may not marry mother, daughter, grandmother, granddaughter, sister, half-sister, aunt, niece, grandaunt, first cousin, grandniece, first cousin once removed.

Vermont

Certificate authorizing marriage issued by clerk of town where man resides; if he is nonresident, by clerk of town where woman resides. If both are nonresidents, by clerk of town where marriage will be solemnized. Cost of license, $6.00. Waiting period after license filed, 5 days. Minimum ages: male, 18; female, 16. Parental consent necessary when male is under 18, female under 18. Blood test required. No marriage of those "non compos mentis." Man may not marry mother, daughter, grandmother, granddaughter, sister, aunt, niece, stepmother, son's wife, grandfather's wife, grandson's wife, wife's mother, stepdaughter, wife's grandmother, wife's granddaughter. The restrictions in these latter cases stands whether the marriage is dissolved by death or by divorce.

Virginia

License issued by clerk of circuit court of county in which female resides; in case she is nonresident, county in which marriage is to be solemnized. Cost of license, $7.00. Minimum ages: male, 18; female, 16. Parental consent necessary when under 21. Blood test required. Surety bond of $500 of clergyman before authorization by circuit court to perform ceremony. No marriage of habitual criminals, idiots, imbeciles, epileptics, insanes, or venereals. Man may not marry mother, daughter, grandmother, granddaughter, sister, half-sister, aunt, niece, stepmother, son's wife, wife's daughter, wife's granddaughter. Prohibition stands in most instances whether the relationship is dissolved by death or divorce.

Washington

License issued by county auditor. Cost of license, $7.00. Waiting period for license, 3 days. Minimum ages: 18 for both parties. Every marriage entered into in which either party has not attained age of 17 shall be void except where 18 year requirement is waived by a superior court judge of county in which the female resides on showing necessity. No blood test required. Two witnesses necessary. No marriage of drunkards, habitual criminals, epileptics, imbeciles, feeble-minded, idiots, insane, venereals, or those afflicted with tuberculosis in an advanced degree, except when woman is forty-five or over. Man may not marry mother, daughter, grandmother, granddaughter, sister, aunt, niece, half-niece, grandaunt, great-grandaunt, first cousin, half-first cousin, grandniece, great-grandniece, first cousin once removed, half-first cousin once removed.

West Virginia

License issued by clerk or county court of county in which female usually resides. Waiting period for license, 3 days. Minimum ages: male, 18; female, 16. Parental consent necessary when under 21. Blood test required. Minister's credentials to perform marriage issued by either circuit or county court. Surety bond of $1,500 required. Man may not marry mother, daughter, grandmother, granddaughter, sister, half-sister, aunt, niece, wife of nephew, first cousin, double first cousin, stepmother, son's wife, wife's daughter, wife's grandmother, wife's granddaughter. Prohibition stands in most cases whether the relationship has been dissolved by divorce or by death. Cost of license: $5.00.

Wisconsin

License issued by clerk of county in which either party resides; if nonresidents, county in which marriage will be solemnized. Cost of license, $5.00. Waiting period for license, 5 days. Minimum ages: male, 18; female, 16. Parental consent necessary when male is under 21, female under 18. Blood test required. Ministers must receive certificate from clerk of circuit court before they are authorized to perform marriage ceremony. Two witnesses necessary. No marriage of idiots, insane, or feeble-minded. Man may not marry mother, daughter, grandmother, granddaughter, sister, aunt, niece, grandaunt, great-grandaunt, second cousin except when female is over fifty-five, grandniece, great-grandniece, second cousin. Marriage of persons nearer of kin than second cousin is prohibited except that first cousins may marry when the woman is over 55 years of age.

Wyoming*

License issued by clerk of county in which marriage is to take place. Minimum ages: male, 18; female, 16. Parental consent necessary when under 21. Blood test required. Two witnesses required. No marriage of venereals. Man may not marry mother, daughter, grandmother, granddaughter, sister, half-sister, aunt, niece. Cost of license: $5.00.

COUNSELING BIBLIOGRAPHY

I. Pastoral Counseling With Couples Before and After the Wedding.

Clinebell, Howard J., Jr. *Basic Types of Pastoral Counseling.* Nashville: Abingdon Press, 1966. This book signaled the great change in pastoral care in light of the new therapies (especially the human potential movement). Offers types of pastoral care designed to help people grow. Gives a well-rounded survey of the whole field of pastoral counseling with chapter six devoted to marriage counseling and eleven to educative counseling (including premarital). Views premarital counseling as basically a teaching ministry.

Emerson, James G. *Divorce, The Church and Remarriage.* Philadelphia: Westminster Press, 1961. A real good solid piece of work which the pastor counseling with divorced persons preparing to remarry will find helpful. May also be given to divorced persons. Obviously recent developments in the field, such as no-fault divorce laws, are not covered.

Gangsei, Lyle B. *Manual for Group Premarital Counseling.* New York: Association Press, 1971. An excellent resource for doing group premarital counseling. Introduction tells how to set up a group. Book deals with eight areas related to marriage, each a potential problem area. Says the purpose of small group discussions on marriage is to prod and guide young adults into thinking and talking about their values and concepts related to marriage.

Klink, Thomas W. *Depth Perspectives in Pastoral Work*. Englewood Cliffs, N.J.: Prentice-Hall, 1965. Chapter seven on "Marriage Processes" is profound and well worth reading for a process approach to marriage. Presents a number of theories of marriage in order to encourage acquiring a wider range of pastoral methods.

Komarovsky, Mirra. *Blue-Collar Marriage*. New York: Vintage Books, 1967, 397 pp. A very penetrating study of marriage relationships in the working-class families of the United States. Uses case study method, and the strong sense of human interest suggests the qualities of the novel. Should be read by anyone interested in the dynamics of working-class marriages.

Oates, Wayne E. *Pastoral Counseling*. Philadelphia: Westminster Press, 1974. Written by one of the leading professors of pastoral care, this book incorporates the best of biblical and psychological insights and relates them to pastoral care. Professor Oates discusses thoroughly the problems connected with pre- and post-marital counseling. Highly recommended for every pastor.

Rutledge, Aaron L. *Pre-Marital Counseling*. Cambridge, Mass.: Schenkman Publishing Co., Inc., 1966. The most extensive book in the field. Claims that premarital counseling is the greatest educational and clinical opportunity in the life of the person. Grew out of the author's extensive experience in marriage counseling and is of special interest to professionals.

Stewart, Charles William. *The Minister as Marriage Counselor*. Nashville: Abingdon Press, 1970. The best available book on pastoral marriage counseling. Should be on every concerned pastor's bookshelf. Sets forth a role-relationship theory of counseling with sufficient case material. Stresses the need for a program of family-life education in each church. Offers practical guidance for pastors seeking to help persons find a faith to give their lives stability and values for living.

II. Resources for Couples Preparing for Marriage

Duvall, Sylvanus M. *Before You Marry*. New York: Association Press, 1959. A book to help young people in the selection of a mate, what to expect in marriage, and how to plan for marriage. Contains help for ministers doing premarital counseling. Should be in every church library.

Hathorn, Raban; Genne, William H.; and Brill, Mordecai L. *Marriage: An Interfaith Guide for All Couples*. New York: Association Press, 1970. Combines the traditions, insights, values, and goals for marriage of the Catholic, Protestant, and Jewish faiths. Illustrated with facts, statistics, cases, and examples. Not primarily directed toward religiously mixed marriages, however.

Mace, David R. *Getting Ready for Marriage*. Nashville: Abingdon Press, 1972. An outstanding book by one of the leaders in the field of marriage counseling. Could be given each couple coming for premarital counseling. Is based on the premise that the best way to prepare a couple for the future is to help them to achieve a successful relationship here and now. Can be used in group premarriage or post-wedding ministry. Was written for couples who do not have the benefit of professional premarriage counseling.

Nelson, Elof G. *Your Life Together*. Richmond: John Knox Press, 1969. Written for young, middle-class, church-related American adults who are considering marriage. Deals with the major areas of married life from a Christian perspective.

To Love and to Cherish (for engaged couples), the marriage manual for The United Methodist Church, and *To Love and to Cherish*, the pastor's manual for premarital counseling in The United Methodist Church. Nashville: The United Methodist Publishing House, 1970. These would be helpful for pastors and couples of any church seriously concerned about marriage preparation.

Pike, James A. *If You Marry Outside Your Faith*. New York: Harper Torchbooks, 1954. Still the best book giving counsel on marrying a person from a different religious faith. Helpful for seminars with young people and in a ministry to those preparing to be married. Should be in every church library.

III. The Sexual Aspect of Marriage

Berne, Eric. *Sex in Human Loving*. New York: Simon and Schuster, 1970. Witty in style and thorough in scope. Recommended for couples wishing to explore sex in marriage from the transactional analysis perspective.

Bird, Joseph W. and Lois F. *The Freedom of Sexual Love*. Garden City: Doubleday & Co., Inc., 1966. Presents the marital union as a commitment in love in which the mystery and meaning of Christian marriage are to be found. One of the best books for exploring the psychological and spiritual aspects of lovemaking and the nature of man and woman as they interact as husband and wife. Affirms that it is love which gives sexuality its beauty and purpose. Candid, explicit, from a Roman Catholic point of view.

Bovet, Theodor. *A Handbook to Marriage*. Garden City: Dolphin Books, 1960. Relates sex in marriage to personal love and religious beliefs. Written by a Swiss doctor and marriage counselor, the book deals with everything from the wedding night to birth control, pregnancy, divorce, and remarriage.

Butterfield, Oliver M. *Sexual Harmony in Marriage*. New York: Emerson Books, 1967. A standard work in the field. Has been used successfully by pastors and marriage counselors in teaching couples how to achieve sexual happiness in marriage.

Family Life Publications, Inc. Box 427, Saluda, NC, 28773. An excellent source of tests, books, and other materials for use in premarital and marriage counseling. Ask for their list of materials and sample copies.

Fisher, Seymour. *The Female Orgasm*. New York: Basic Books, Inc., 1973. The most exhaustive study of the subject from the psychological dimension. Done over a five-year period with a grant from the National Institute of Mental Health, the research involved interviewing three hundred middle-class wives. Reveals the relationship between personality and sexual responsiveness with special attention given to personal traits which are correlated with orgasm capacity.

Goldstein, Martin; Haeberle, Edwin J.; and McBride, Will. *The Sex Book.* New York: Herder and Herder, Inc., 1971. A comprehensive photo-illustrated encyclopedia with up-to-date medical views, Christian sexual and family morality. Looks upon sex and the human body as natural and beautiful. Designed to appeal to today's visually oriented youth and to mature adults interested in a modern approach to sex education.

Lewin, S. A., and Gilmore, John. *Sex Without Fear.* New York: Medical Research Press, 1970. A standard resource for sex education prepared by doctors. Simple and clear. Presents medically, psychologically, and ethically correct information. Illustrations are clear, precise, and in good taste.

Packard, Vance. *The Sexual Wilderness.* New York: David McKay Co., Inc., 1968. Surveys the changes and new problems in human sexuality, including trends in premarital intimacy. Outlines the shifting roles of husbands and wives. Very helpful assessment of situation and suggests possible directions for the future.

IV. Especially for Newlyweds

Adams, Theodore F. *Making Your Marriage Succeed.* New York: Harper & Brothers, 1953. Written by a leading Baptist pastor out of many years of marriage counseling experiences. Offers wise counsel to couples in various periods of married life.

Bach, George R., and Wyden, Peter. *The Intimate Enemy*. New York: Avon Books, 1968. Asserts that couples who fight fairly together are couples who stay together. In their successful marriage counseling practice, the authors teach couples the art of fighting properly. Fair fighting demands hearts and minds open—open to reason and change.

Clinebell, Charlotte Holt, *Meet Me in the Middle/On Being Human Together*. New York: Harper & Row Publishers, 1973. Written in light of women's liberation this book spells out what freedom means for both wife and husband. Offers a nonradical application of freedom to the dilemma of the modern woman. A chapter by the author's husband gives his reactions to the changes that have occurred to his wife and their marriage.

Clinebell, Howard J. *The People Dynamic*. New York: Harper and Row, 1972. The author says that growth groups seem to be the most effective means for the maximum number of persons to experience enlivening within themselves and in their relationships with others. Tells how to tap the people dynamic—the power we have to re-create each other and ourselves through caring and sharing. Would be a very helpful book in developing a ministry to newlyweds.

Duvall, Evelyn M., and Hill, Reuben. *Being Married*. New York: Association Press, 1960. A very practical book for those preparing for marriage or already married by two of America's leading authorities in family and marriage.

Fairchild, Roy W. *Christians in Families*. Richmond: CLC Press, 1964. A splendid Christian interpretation of the nature and mission of the family. Provides resources to assist families to live under the Lordship of Christ. Note especially chapters three and four on marriage through the eyes of faith and the challenge of the sexual revolution.

Fromm, Erich. *The Art of Loving*. New York: Bantam Books, 1962. One of the best basic statements of the problems of human relations. Tells how to make love become the most exhilarating and exciting experience of life. Shows how to overcome the fear of love and to use love to conquer shame and anxiety.

Hovde, Howard. *The Neo-Married*. Valley Forge: The Judson Press, 1968. Offers a series of study plans for a group of newlyweds who want to explore further the experience of living in the covenant relationship of marriage. Sound in theology and ideas and yet practical in application. A unique book in the field of pastoral care.

McGinnis, Tom. *Your First Year of Marriage*. Garden City: Doubleday & Co., Inc., 1967. Argues that the first year is the crucial year of marriage, when patterns of feeling, thinking, and acting are developed and tend to persist. Explains how a couple can learn to understand the emotional factors which affect their relationship and can communicate better their true feelings.

O'Neill, Nena and George. *Open Marriage*. New York: Avon Books, 1972. Stresses the need for trust, liking, role flexibility, individual freedom and growth, love and sex without jealousy. A widely read book, it would need to be supplemented with a Christian doctrine of marriage for use in church groups.

V. Marriage in the Middlescent Years

Lee, Robert and Casebier, Marjorie. *The Spouse Gap.* Nashville: Abingdon Press, 1971. Seeks to stimulate recognition and reflection and to shed light on middlescent malaise. A "self-help" book that is thoroughly honest in its approach to problems and possibilities of marriage.

VI. Marriage in General

Bowman, Henry A. *Marriage for Moderns.* New York: McGraw-Hill, 6th ed., 1970. One of the best comprehensive sources of information and guidance for couples today. Covers all the major areas of marriage and has been used for years as a textbook for college-level courses on marriage. Should be in every church library.

Capon, Robert Farrar. *Bed and Board.* New York: Simon and Schuster, 1965. A very witty, entertaining but practical book about marriage and life. Written by a priest of the Episcopal Church who is happily married and who shares out of his experience and observation the joys and pitfalls of marriage.

Clinebell, Charlotte H. and Howard J. *The Intimate Marriage.* New York: Harper & Row, 1970. Emphasizes the companion aspect of marriage. Written by a husband and wife team who are recognized authorities on marriage counseling and who are able to communicate effectively from their experience in counseling and out of their own marriage.

Howe, Reuel L. *The Miracle of Dialogue.* New

York: Seabury Press, 1963. Howe says that by dialogue we can let God into our world because in dialogue we open ourselves to one another and to God. The miracle of dialogue is that it can renew a relationship that had died. An excellent book for couples preparing for marriage or those seeking to renew their marriage.

Hudson, R. Lofton. *Til Divorce Do Us Part*. New York: Thos. Nelson Co., 1973. Has been used effectively with marriage growth groups to enable couples to explore the dynamics of the marriage relationship. Recognizes the forces at work in contemporary society to destroy marriages and discusses ways to prevent marriage break-ups.

Lederer, William J., and Jackson, Don D. *The Mirages of Marriage*. New York: W. W. Norton & Co., Inc., 1968. Deals with the techniques of appraising one's own marriage, the use of counselors, the dangers of unilateral therapy, and the major elements of a satisfactory marriage. The book is based on the premise that marriage is a system in which the partners act and react to each other and to the total relationship in definable ways. Claims that husband and wife in an unhappy marriage can do the greater part of the healing and growing for themselves.

May, Rollo. *Love and Will*. New York: W. W. Norton and Co., 1969. An excellent book on the subject by one of America's leading psycho-analysts. His treatment of sex in marriage is especially helpful.

Shedd, Charlie, W. *Letters to Karen*. New York: Avon Books, 1968. Very readable letters from a pastor-father to his married daughter discussing problems of marriage and offering practical advice on real needs in marriage. Full of parental affection and religious faith. Written out of twenty-five years' pastoral experience.

Shedd, Charlie W. *Letters to Philip*. Old Tappan, N.J.: Fleming H. Revell Company, 1969. A sequel to *Letters to Karen*. Written to the author's son to give experience-tested advice about dealing with members of the opposite sex. Tells about everything any man needs to know to make him a better husband, keep his wife happy, and bring them success in marriage.

VII. Family Budgets

The Rubber Budget Account Book. Order from "American Institute For Economic Research," Great Barrington, Mass. Ask for list of other materials available.

VIII. Devotional Life

Barclay, William. *Daily Celebrations*. Waco: Word Books, 1973. Written by one of the best known writers in the English speaking Christian community, this book is fresh and readable. It draws from the wealth of the best writers of the past and present on a wide range of topics. An excellent book to help any couple begin a devotional life.

Mace, David R. *Whom God Hath Joined*. Philadelphia: Westminster Press, 1953. A book of daily readings to be used by a husband and wife for their first month of married life.

Snyder, Ross. *Inscape*. Nashville: Abingdon Press,

1968. A delightful book in poetic form and insight to help couples grasp the potential of life and marriage. A book to be read and reread to help couples experience love and marriage and creation at the deepest levels of their being.

IX. Prenuptial Contracts

Sheresky, Norman, and Mannes, Marya. *Uncoupling.* New York: Dell Publishing Co., Inc., 1972. Chapter 2 contains an excellent example of a prenuptial agreement (pp. 33-49). Written as a guide for those divorcing, this book could help those contemplating marriage or already married to take a more serious look at their marriage contract. The model marriage contract could help couples clarify their own contract and thus prevent later misunderstandings and divorce.

INDEX

Ministry after wedding, 14, 18, 23-31
  early months crucial to, 23-25
  group seminars for, 27-30
  neglected, 24, 25
  resources for, 25, 26

National Presbyterian Mariners, 27
Negative feelings, 19

Parents, 18, 19, 29, 34, 53, 54. *See also* Family ties
Participation by congregation, 38, 88, 109, 110
Photographer, 101, 102, 111, 115
Poetry, 32, 48
Prayer bench, 73, 110
Premarital counseling, 12-15, 23, 31
  assumptions in, 16, 17
  expected, 13
  flexibility in, 17, 21, 22
  goals for, 17, 18
  group, 21, 22
  number of interviews in, 18
  obstacles to, 14, 15

Premarital counseling—*cont'd*
  outline for, 20, 21
  values questioned, 13, 14
Preceremony music, 89
Previously married, 19. *See also* Divorce

Realized forgiveness, 19
Rehearsal, 18, 58
  beginning the, 62
  as directed by minister, 58-60, 112
  length of, 62
  overview of, 63, 64
  place for, 62
  planning for, 60, 61
  prayer at, 63
  procedure for, 77, 78
  time for, 61, 62
Ring and the Book, The, 27, 28
Ring(s), 52, 72-76
Rite of passage, 34, 54

Sacraments, 11. *See also* Lord's Supper
Scripture, 32, 57
Secular music, 84, 86, 87
Self-identity, 33
Sermon (homily), 11, 34, 38-40, 42, 43